# Collecting Rock 'n' Roll Sheet Music of the 1960s

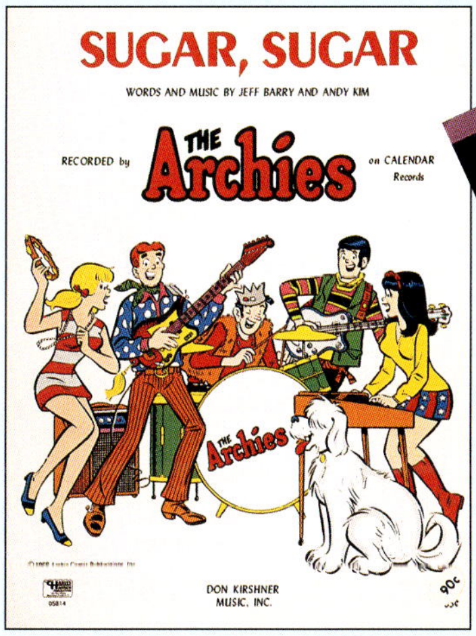

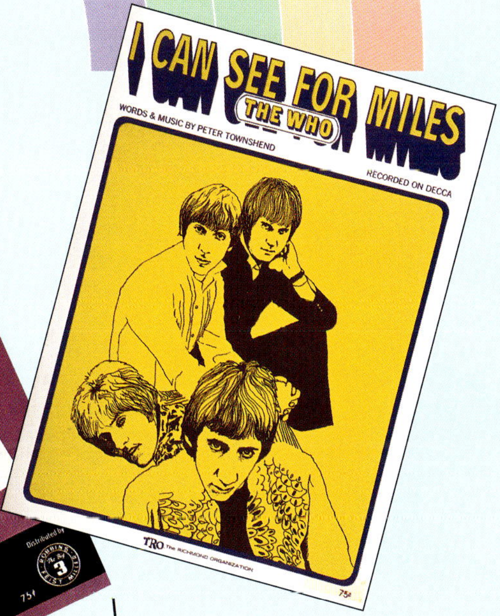

Valerie Carallo

Schiffer Publishing Ltd®
4880 Lower Valley Road, Atglen, PA 19310 US.

# Dedication

This book is dedicated to my Mom, Dad, family, and friends who were there for me during the tough times. Your support and love have given me the independence, courage, and strength to achieve anything I put my mind to, including something as wonderful as this book.

Library of Congress Cataloging-in-Publication Data

Carallo, Valerie.
Collecting rock 'n' roll : sheet music of the 1960s / Valerie Carallo.
p. cm.
Includes bibliographical references and index.
ISBN 0-7643-2373-3 (soft cover)
1. Rock music—1961-1970—Collectibles. I. Title.

ML3534.C29 2006
781.66026'3075—dc22

2005028194



Designed by Mark David Bowyer
Type set in Van Dijk / Souvenir Lt BT

ISBN: 0-7643-2373-3
Printed in China
1 2 3 4



Published by Schiffer Publishing Ltd.
4880 Lower Valley Road
Atglen, PA 19310
Phone: (610) 593-1777; Fax: (610) 593-2002
E-mail: Info@schifferbooks.com

For the largest selection of fine reference books on this and related subjects, please visit our web site at
**www.schifferbooks.com**
We are always looking for people to write books on new and related subjects. If you have an idea for a book please contact us at the above address.

This book may be purchased from the publisher.
Include $3.95 for shipping.
Please try your bookstore first.
You may write for a free catalog.

In Europe, Schiffer books are distributed by
Bushwood Books
6 Marksbury Ave.
Kew Gardens
Surrey TW9 4JF England
Phone: 44 (0) 20 8392-8585; Fax: 44 (0) 20 8392-9876
E-mail: info@bushwoodbooks.co.uk
Free postage in the U.K., Europe; air mail at cost.

# Contents

Recorded by NEIL DIAMOND on BANG RECORDS
CHERRY, CHERRY
Words and Music by NEIL DIAMOND

CREEQUE ALLEY

PIECE OF MY HEART

# Acknowledgments

I would like to thank my Mom for proofreading, helping with the photos, and in general for listening to me prattle on endlessly about this book and its possibilities—I am grateful beyond words; Bob Foetsch from The Pastrami Malted for the invaluable information about his band; Michael Capoziello for sharing his vast Herb Alpert knowledge; the members of the bulletin boards of http://www.oldiesmusic.com and http://groups.msn.com/PSPOT—your extensive knowledge and generosity in taking the time to answer my questions is greatly appreciated; and to all the sheet music dealers I've had the pleasure of buying from—it was really all of you who made this book possible! Thank you!

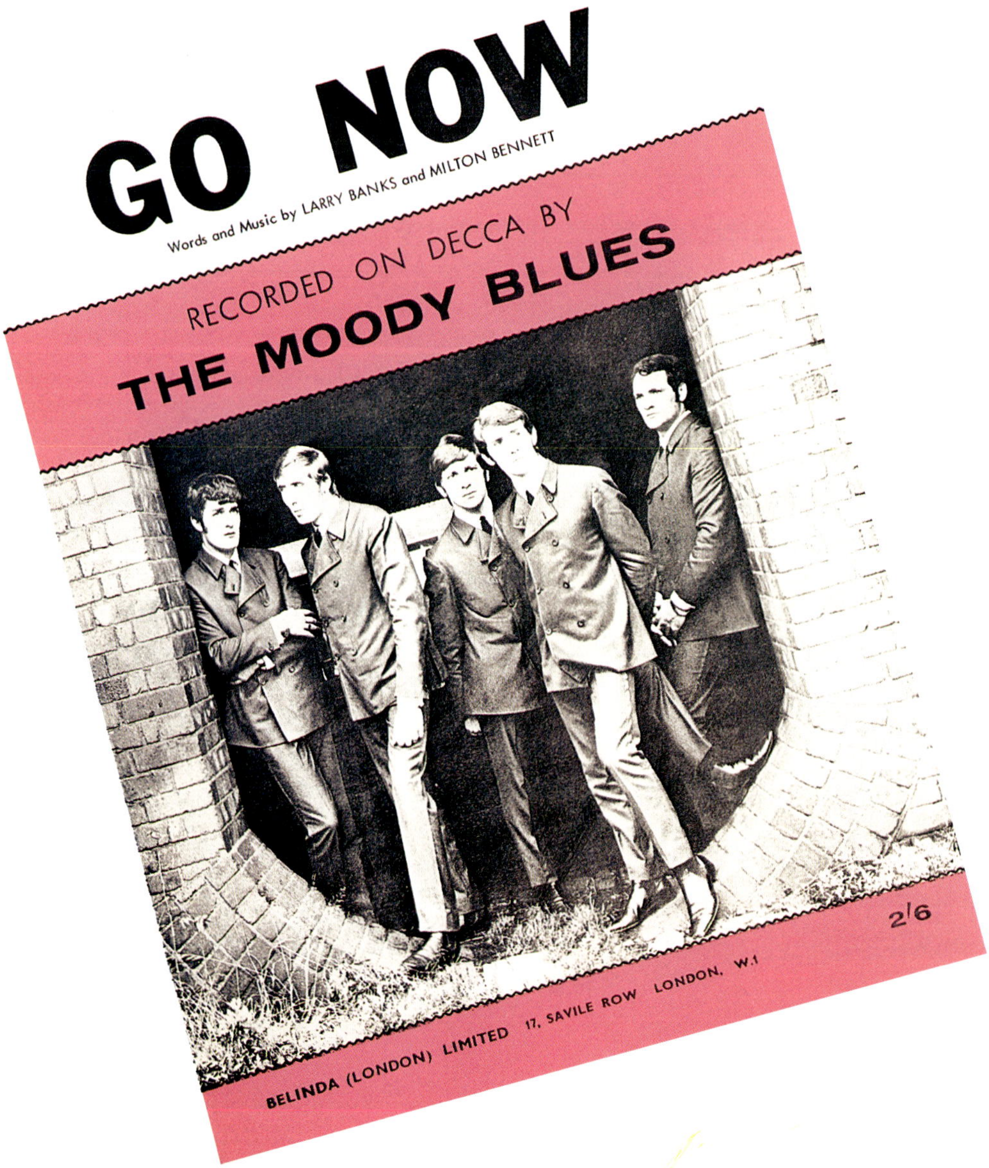

# Introduction

Sheet music is plainly defined as a musical composition in printed or written form[1]—if it were only that simple! These often forgotten bits of memorabilia are fantastic time capsules to an era gone by. They show hairstyles, fashions, and sometimes dances that were popular at the time. Even the colors and graphics used to design the covers will be a reflection of popular tastes. If you like 1960s rock and roll, collecting sheet music is a great way to take your enjoyment of that music a step further.

Some people collect rock and pop sheet music as a fascination all its own, but most people who collect it are typically supplementing an already existing collection of records or other memorabilia, whether focused on a specific group or a particular style. For the most part, no one is buying forty-year-old sheet music just so they can play it on their guitar at home. It's collectible for the picture that appears on the front cover and because it's an original piece of the past. Collecting sheet music for its own sake does have some appealing points—it's easy to store, looks great when displayed, and many pieces are available at reasonable prices. Who could ask for more?

The rock and roll sheet music hobby is still a relatively low key one—unlike record collecting, for example, which is highly visible. If you were to collect records, you would have magazines, websites, numerous books, and an untold amount of antique shows, flea markets, and garage sales where you can find your treasures. With sheet music, you'll have to work a little harder.

As it turns out, record websites and magazines are good places to start looking. In magazines, be sure to check the bottoms of ads, and on websites you should look under "Memorabilia," "Paper Items," or "Miscellaneous."

As a rule, sheet music from the 1960s consisted of one large piece of paper with a fold down the center. It had a picture on the front, music on the inside, and lyrics or an advertisement printed on the back. However, sometimes you get a bonus and there is an extra sheet or insert included. Usually it's there because additional room was needed for the music, for a dance that accompanied the song, or to show the same song arranged for another instrument. Because these inserts are not attached to the cover they can get lost, so it is important to count the page numbers to be certain the sheet is complete.

All sheet music pictured in this book was printed in the United States unless otherwise mentioned. In addition, there are no sheet music books or folios here, only individual songs. Please note that I have attempted to sort all of the sheets into neat little chapters arranged by genre, but anyone who knows rock and roll knows how difficult it can sometimes be to classify. If there's a group or artist that you don't feel quite belongs in the chapter where it was placed, please remember that much music classification is subjective. Many groups and solo artists changed their sound as different songs were released, and often an individual song can contain influences from multiple sources.

There are three main places that printed the sheet music contained in this book: The United States, The United Kingdom, and Australia. Each has traits and characteristics that are unique to that location. Some general descriptions are given below to help you understand what is standard and what is unusual. There are, of course, a few exceptions, but this is mostly what you'll find.

As for sheet music from places other than the three mentioned here, not enough sufficient examples are available at this time to make determinations about what is standard.

## United States Sheet Music

Sheet music from the United States is very creative and varied. It could have been printed in one color or in full color, with different weights of paper, or with a glossy or matte cover. The finished product was even created in different sizes: a small 8.5" x 11" size and a standard 9" x 12" size.

While the 9" x 12" size has been printed for many years—and is still being printed today— the smaller 8.5" x 11" size seems to only have been printed in the U.S. from about the early 1960s to the mid 1970s. Before that, there was only the 9" x 12" size and before that they were 11" x 14"!

The small sheets were normally printed on a matte, medium weight paper or sometimes a sturdy card stock. Occasionally, some were printed on a thinner paper, with a glossy finish. The standard 9" x 12" size used the lighter weight paper most of the time and almost always had a glossy finish to the cover.

The cover styles were also quite interesting, using not only artist photos but graphics as well. Graphics are the descriptive drawings or colorful lines, swirls, and shapes that surround a band photo and in some cases, are used instead of one. Often the drawings didn't just decorate the sheet music, they helped explain it. For instance, "Young Girl" by The Union Gap has a childlike drawing of a little girl, while "Green Tambourine" by The Lemon Pipers actually has a drawing of, you guessed it, a green tambourine. As simplistic as these drawings can be, those designs are sometimes one of the best aspects of the sheet music—they really give a feeling of the innocence of the time.

While the covers could have been printed in any combination of ink colors, from just one color to all or full color, the music inside was almost always printed in black ink no matter what colors were used on the outside. Sheet music with full color covers could be found now and then in the U.S. on both the small and large sizes. However, it wasn't common on either size (it was a costly process) and you see it more regularly on the smaller size.

The 9" x 12" sheets were known for having the cover printed in only one color. Photos, words, and everything else found on the cover, would have been done in one color ink only.

Using a photograph of the band combined with an interesting graphic was characteristic of U.S. sheet music in the Sixties.

An excellent example of full color U.S. sheet music using an artist photograph on the cover.

This example of U.S. sheet music, using only graphics on the cover, precisely illustrates the title of the song.

## *United Kingdom Sheet Music*

As innovators of popular music of the time, the United Kingdom was prolific in their printing of sheet music during the 1960s. There is so much available today, it is a virtual goldmine for collectors. The cover layouts are different, the colors are different, the photos are different, and you can find sheets for many obscure bands and songs that were not very popular in America at that time.

The vast majority of U.K. sheets were printed using a "two-color" printing process—black ink for the photo (normally known as black and white) and a second color to accent the sheet. It is very unusual to see sheet music from the United Kingdom printed in full color. Although it has happened, it is exceptionally rare.

All U.K. sheets are printed in the 8.5" x 11" format. Sometimes, due to irregularities in the printing process, some sheets are just a bit larger or smaller than 8.5" x 11", but this is not a specific size, just an exception.

On sheet music from the United Kingdom, it is uncommon to find any kind of graphics, as in a design or drawing, the way they are frequently seen on sheet music from the United States. Now and then simple drawings were used, but not to the degree or with the importance that occurred in the United States. In general, there was very little extra decoration to the cover design. It normally consisted of the photo in black and white with some large, simple areas of color around it.

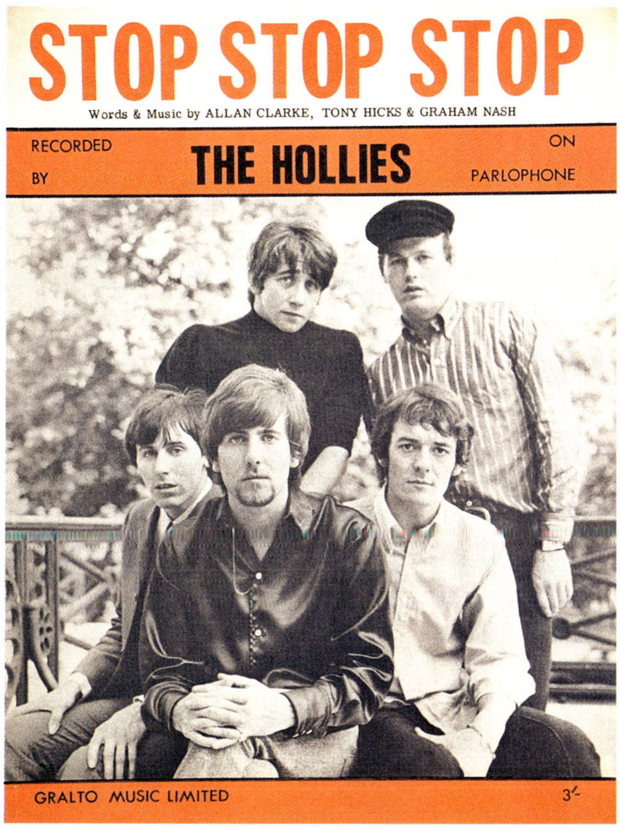


Sample of standard U.K. sheet music using a black and white photo plus an accent color for the title and colored bands.

## *Australian Sheet Music*

More often than not, sheet music printed in Australia was done in a simple way using only one color ink to print the whole cover. Once in a while, you will find printing with two colors, but it is not as common as the single color. Also, the same photo that was used on a U.S. or U.K. sheet was sometimes used again on an Australian sheet. For this reason, a number of these sheets are not very visually exciting, but when you do find one that is different or unusual, it is quite a treasure!

As for size, you will only find the smaller 8.5" x 11" size used for Australian sheet music; the larger 9" x 12" size was not printed in that country at that time.

This example was printed with one color ink only, which was typical of Australian sheet music.

## *Dating Vintage Sheet Music*

How do you tell how old a piece of sheet music is or when it was printed? Well, sheet music from the 1960s came in different sizes, different weights of paper, and both glossy and matte finishes, so unfortunately, there is no way to use any of that as a guide. In addition, copyright date is NOT a good way to tell the age of a piece of sheet music. For example, an old song such as "Yesterday" by The Beatles is regularly published to sell to today's musicians. It will state "© 1965" no matter when it's printed. You may even find an old photo on the front cover. To add to the confusion, many tunes are new recordings of an older song. These will have a copyright date that can be much older than when the sheet was printed. For example, "Unchained Melody" by The Righteous Brothers was a number four hit for them in 1965, but the sheet music says © 1955. The moral? Never use copyright date as the sole factor in determining the age of a piece of sheet music.

So, how do you tell what is vintage and what is modern? There are two good ways. The first is by the date code on the back, bottom right hand side of the sheet. This date code can be found on the back of the small U.S. sheets, and consists of a few numbers that look something like this: 568/M/16366. The first set of numbers is actually the month and year that piece of sheet music was printed, in this case, May 1968. This is a great way of telling not only the age of a sheet, but also which of two copies of the same song with different cover photos was printed first. However, these numbers *only* appear on U.S. sheets in the 8.5" x 11" size. They do not appear on the 9" x 12" size or any of the foreign printings.

The second way to tell the age of a piece of sheet music is by the price. This means the **original selling price** printed on the front of the sheet music, not the price from a price sticker or rubber stamp and certainly not the selling price a dealer is asking. Here is a time when inflation, for once, can be your friend. The lower the price, the older the sheet—all you need to know is what a sheet sold for in a given year and when the prices went up.

As a rule, sheet music printed in the U.S. during the 1960s would have a selling price of 75¢, with sheets from the earlier part of the decade having a price of 60¢ and those towards the end of the decade selling for a bit more. The original selling price for United Kingdom sheet music at that time was normally between £2'6 or £3/—this is read as "two shillings & sixpence" or "three shillings." For Australian sheet music, the original selling price was listed as .35 or 40 cents—this, of course, is in Australian dollars and is not to be confused with American dollars.

Here's a little chart to get you started:*

| Years | US | UK | Australia |
|---|---|---|---|
| 1958-1963 | 60¢ | £2/. or £2.6 | .35 |
| 1964-1967 | 75¢ | £3/. | .40 |
| 1968-1969 | 85¢ | £3/. | .45 |
| 1970 | $1.00 | £4/. or 20p | ? |

*All beginning and ending dates are approximate; different publishers may have raised their prices at different times.

## Value & Condition

Values in this book were compiled from standard auctions, Internet auctions, set sales, and the author's own research and experience. Sometimes they can be somewhat higher or lower than what is quoted here, depending on where the sheet is bought or sold. For example, online auctions are making many previously hard to find pieces readily available, occasionally lowering the price. On the other hand, antique dealers have time and overhead to factor into the cost, perhaps making a piece cost a bit more than it normally would. As much as possible, these varying conditions were taken into account when determining the value of a specific piece.

A few different factors can affect the value of a piece of sheet music:

**1) Desirability.** There are various qualities that may increase the desirability of sheet music:

- *Song title*: Hits can be just as sought after as album cuts.
- *Cover photo*: Photo should be different and not appear everywhere the band is mentioned.
- *Artist's popularity*: Artist should have a hit, a respected body of work, or a strong fan base.

**2) Condition.** The better the condition, the more the sheet music will be worth. Paper is so easily damaged, only those pieces of sheet music that show little to no signs of wear—such as those that would be considered in excellent or near mint condition—will deserve high prices.

**3) Rarity**. The less frequently an item appears for sale the more coveted it can be, raising the value. For example, The Beatles are a very desirable band, but some songs are so popular, the sheet music is too common to command a high price. But please note, just because a sheet is rare does not necessarily make it valuable. It may be rare because the song was unpopular and didn't sell well at the time of its release. If the artist is obscure, their sheet music is generally not going to be sought after by many people.

**The values shown in this book are for pieces of sheet music in "near mint" or "excellent" condition, not necessarily for the example pictured. These conditions are defined as follows:**

**Near Mint:** Almost as perfect as the day it was created and without any defects—usually the highest rating a piece of sheet music can receive. Also known as "M-" or mint minus. Many collectors, the author included, do not use the term "Mint" as there is always some aging to a piece of paper that is decades old, even if it is barely perceptible.

**Excellent:** Just a step below near mint. Sheet music in excellent condition will show some minor defects such as gently rounded corners, some light wrinkles, or some mild yellowing due to age, but nothing more. Many collectors term this grade "VG+" or very good plus.

Chapter One

# "Twist and Shout"

## The Beatles

There's little that can be said about The Beatles that hasn't already been said. They were the biggest and most influential band to come out of the 1960s. Nearly all memorabilia related to them is considered desirable and is normally a good investment. They're in a class by themselves musically and that goes for their sheet music as well. A prolific amount of sheet music was published for Beatles songs in the United States, the United Kingdom, and around the world. The prices paid for Beatles sheet music are consistently higher than those paid for sheet music from other groups. Even a common Beatles sheet will cost more than a comparable sheet from any other band.

"A Hard Day's Night" – The Beatles. Title song to The Beatles' first movie in 1964 showing a still from the film itself. A second, more common printing of this sheet music shows pictures from the cover of the album of the same name. 8.5" x 11", $40-60.

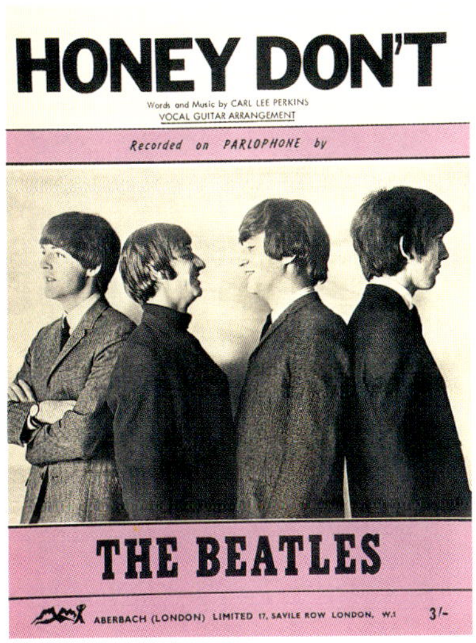


"Honey Don't" (U.K.) – The Beatles. This Beatles recording of the Carl Perkins original was printed in 1964. This is a United Kingdom only printing; there is no sheet music counterpart in the United States. 8.5" x 11", $60-80.

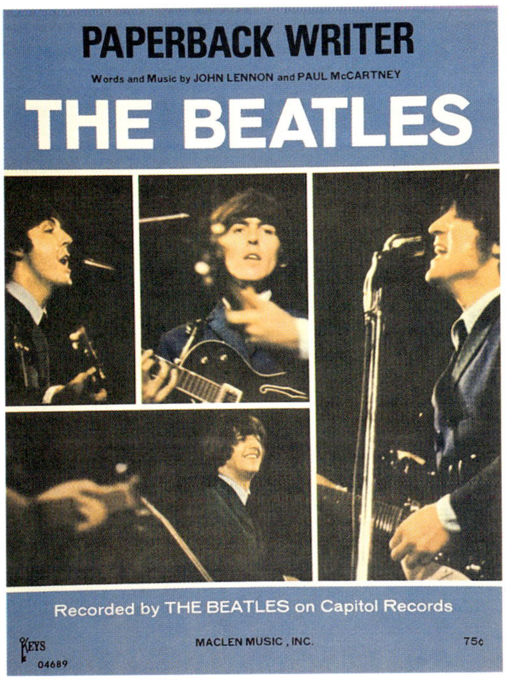


"Paperback Writer" – The Beatles. Beautiful full color cover that features individual, in concert shots of all four Beatles. The same photo layout was used on the picture sleeve for the 7" vinyl single. 8.5" x 11", $35-50.

"I Feel Fine" – The Beatles. Great live photo taken from their performance on *The Ed Sullivan Show* in 1964. This particular sheet is a vintage reprint as indicated by the 09999 number stamped in the bottom left corner. 8.5" x 11", $35-45.

"I Feel Fine" (Spain) – The Beatles. This sheet was originally authorized for sale in Spain and Portugal and shows the song title in Spanish, "Me Siento Feliz," as well as the English translation. The lyrics are also written in both Spanish and English. It is printed on lightweight, newsprint type paper. 8.5" x 12", very rare, $20-30.

"Dear Prudence" (U.K.) – The Beatles. Many sheets printed in the U.K. for songs from *The White Album* use this layout, which features all four individual photos included within the album. The sheet pictured here is a reproduction. 8.5" x 11", $5-10.

"Kansas City" – The Beatles. The picture for The Beatles version of this Leiber and Stoller composition shows a very casual group shot of the boys outside on a sunny day. Printed in February of 1965. 8.5" x 11", $50-75.

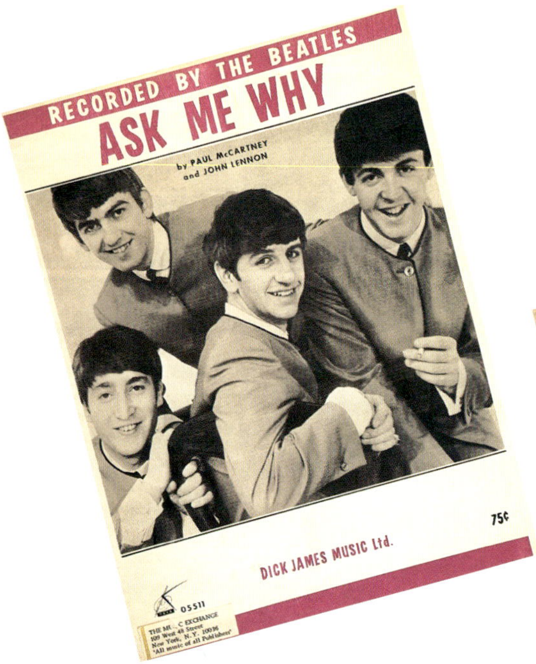


"Ask Me Why" – The Beatles. Familiar Dezo Hoffman photo for a song from the *Meet The Beatles* album. 8.5" x 11", $35-50.

"Let's Kick" (U.K.) – Joe Loss. At the height of their popularity, images of The Beatles were used to promote almost everything, even other people's music. Here, The Beatles, along with a few mod birds, perform a dance known as "The Kick" on a British television program called *Blackpool Night Out*. 8.5" x 11", $25-40.

"A Day in the Life" – The Beatles. The U.S. sheet music for each of the songs issued from The Beatles landmark 1967 album *Sgt. Pepper's Lonely Hearts Club Band* features this same photo. They are the only U.S. sheets issued at the time to show The Beatles in their Sgt. Pepper uniforms. 8.5" x 11", $45-60.

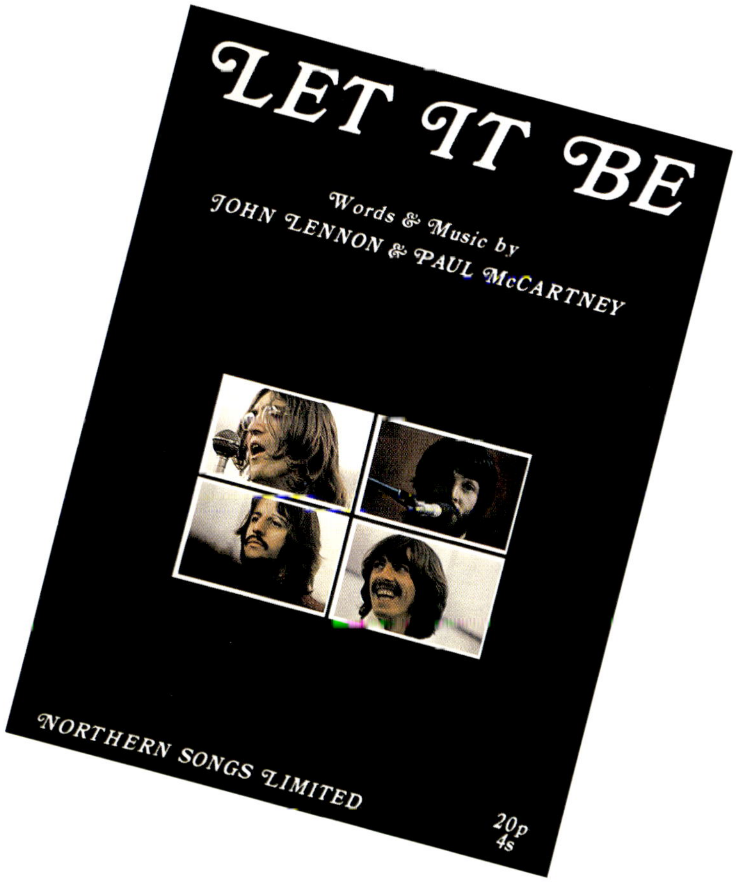


"Let It Be" (U.K.) – The Beatles. Recent reproduction of the original U.K. sheet with elongated pictures taken from the *Let it Be* album cover. 8.5" x 11", $5-10.

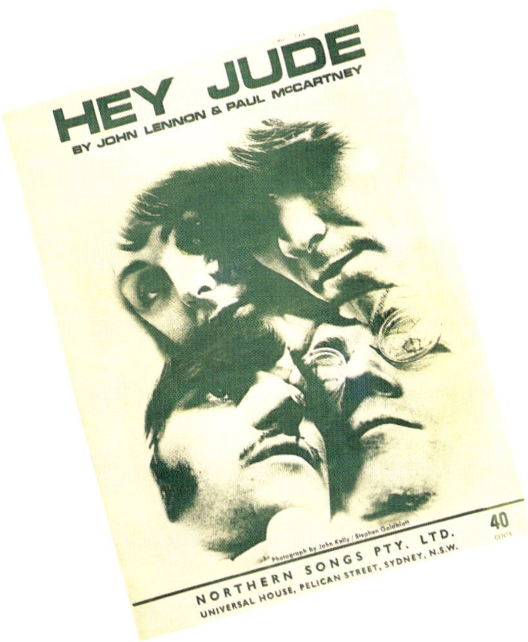


"Hey Jude" (Australia) – The Beatles. Australian version of one of The Beatles' biggest hits. The same image, in black and white, was used on sheets printed in the United Kingdom. 8.5" x 11", $15-25.

"Let It Be" – The Beatles. With a photo that duplicates the album cover, this song sheet was released in 1970, as the $1.00 original selling price indicates. 8.5" x 11", $20-30.

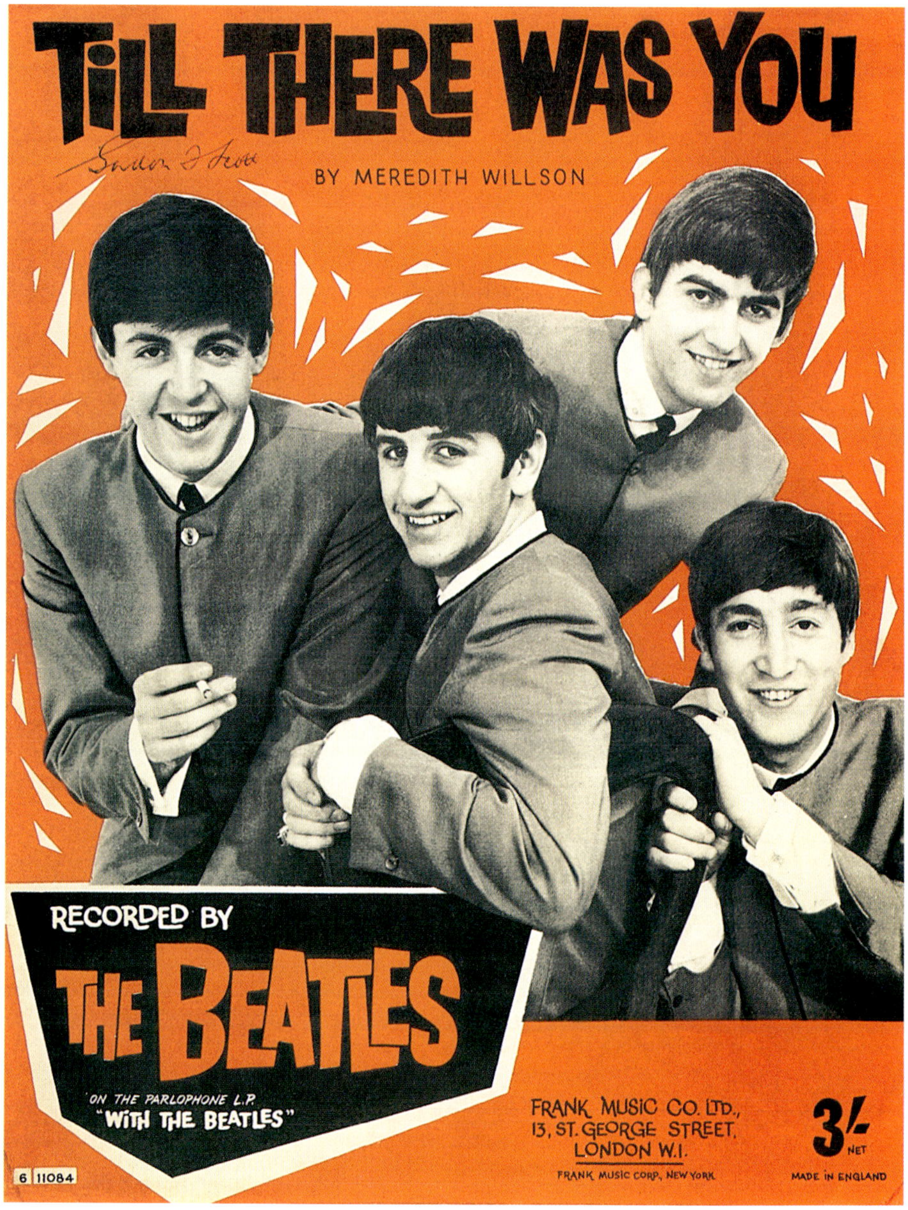


"Till There Was You" (U.K.) – The Beatles. This sheet music is from 1963 for a song that originally appeared in the musical *The Music Man*. The Australian version features the same cover, only with a yellow background. 8.5" x 11", $35-45.

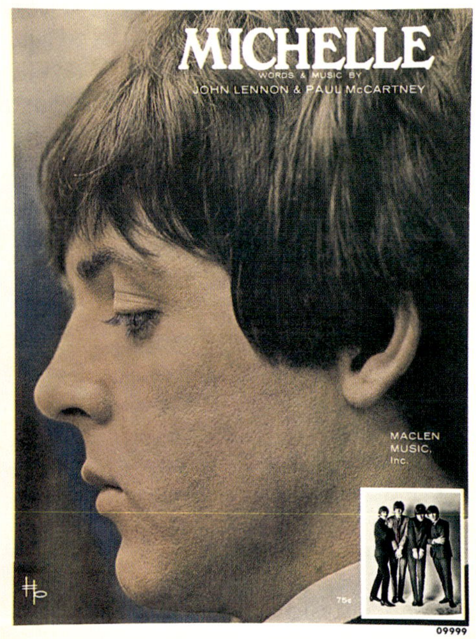


"Michelle" – The Beatles. The cover shows a large, close-up photo of Paul McCartney and also a much smaller shot of the group as a whole. The sheet music for "Yesterday" uses this same cover. 8.5" x 11", $20-35.

"Michelle" (U.K.) – The Beatles. From the *Rubber Soul* LP showing an early posed shot of the fab four in a photo taken by Robert Whitaker. 8.5" x 11", $25-35.

Inset photo from the covers of "Michelle" and "Yesterday." Actual size is about 1.75" x 2.25".

"She's a Woman" (Holland) – The Beatles. This Dutch sheet music features a "cut and paste" version of a Dezo Hoffman photo where the positions of Ringo and John have been switched. 8.75" x 12", very rare, $25-35.

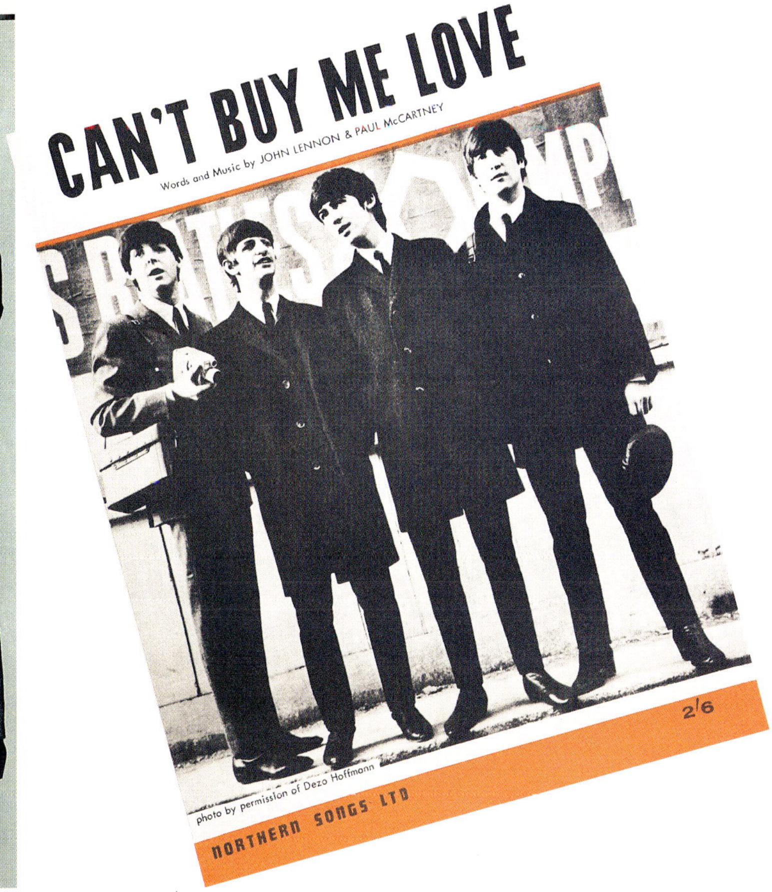


"Can't Buy Me Love" (U.K.) – The Beatles. A number one hit in 1964, this reproduction is adorned with a Dezo Hoffman photo. 8.5" x 11", $5-10.

"Lady Madonna" (Australia) – The Beatles. The ornate typestyle used for the title, as well as the writer credits, adds interest to this single color sheet. 8.5" x 11", $15-20.

"Get Back" (U.K.) – The Beatles. This particular sheet is a reproduction of a later printing. The first printings show an original selling price of £3/- or three shillings, while this one shows the selling price listed as £4/- or 20 pence. 8.5" x 11", $5-10.

"I Want To Hold Your Hand" – The Beatles. The first single released in America; it went to number one in 1964. This early sheet shows an original selling price of only 60¢. 9" x 12", $40-50.

"Penny Lane" (Italy) – The Beatles. This 1967 Italian original depicts the same photo as its U.K. counterpart. The lyrics printed with the music are in both English and Italian. 9.25" x 12", very rare, $20-30.

"Got To Get You Into My Life" (U.K.) – The Beatles. Cover design created by Klaus Voorman, Beatle buddy from the group's early days in Germany. Mr. Voorman also created the cover of the *Revolver* album. 8.5" x 11", $30-40.

"I Want To Hold Your Hand" (Spain) – The Beatles. This sheet was originally authorized for sale in Spain and Portugal and shows the song title in Spanish two different ways, "Tu Mano Cogere" and "Quiero Coger Tu Mano," as well as the English translation. The lyrics that accompany the music are written in Spanish. The English lyrics are printed separately on the back. 8.75" x 12", very rare, $20-30.

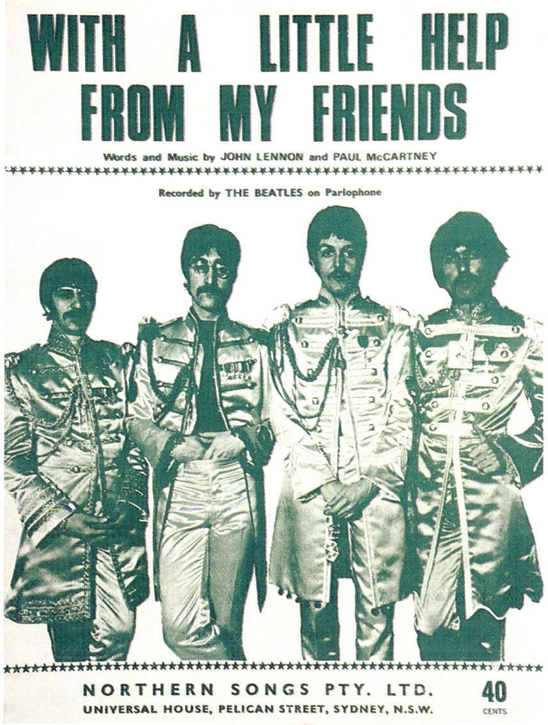


"With a Little Help From My Friends" (Australia) – The Beatles. Single color printing of The Beatles in their classic Sgt. Pepper uniforms. 8.5" x 11", $15-20.

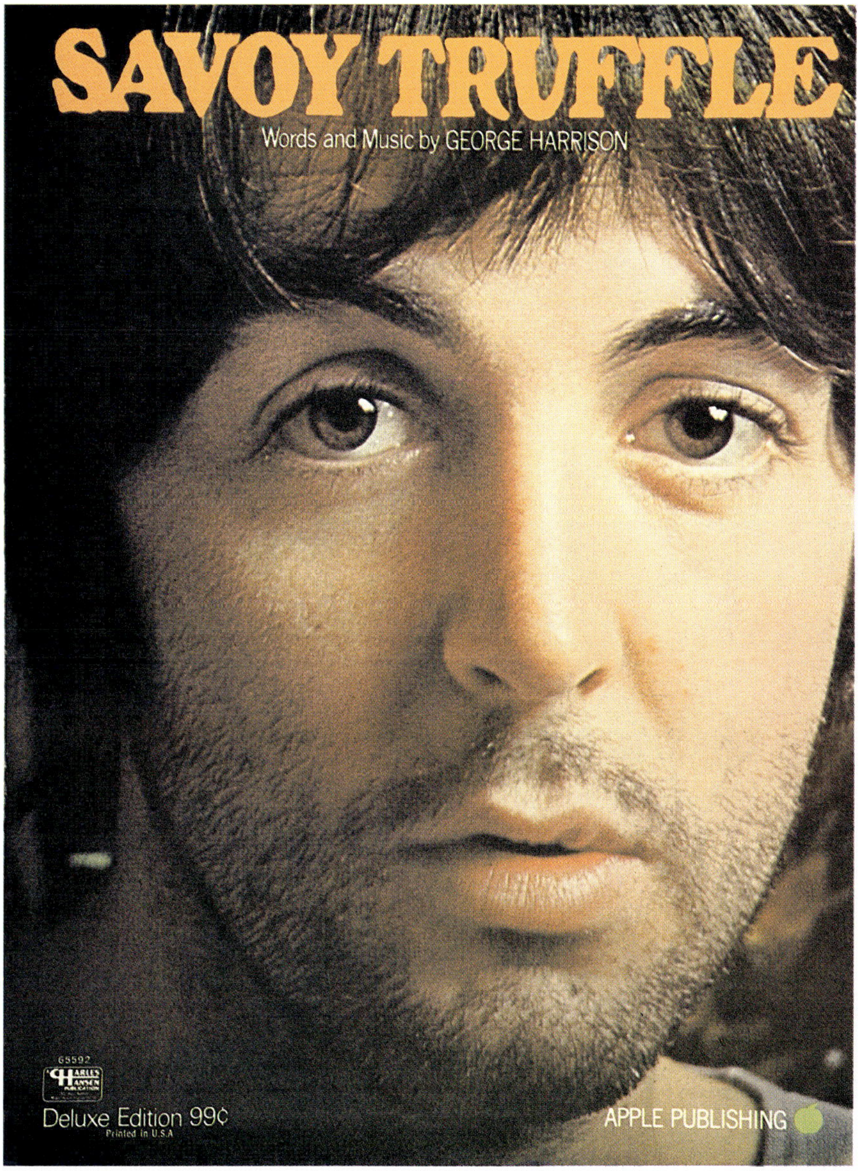


"Savoy Truffle" – The Beatles. A full color, full-page photo of Paul McCartney was used on this 1968 George Harrison composition. There are eight pages altogether, including a line drawing of two girls, a casual photo of George, three pages of music, the lyrics written on a separate page without the music, and the four full color *White Album* shots of the fabs on the back. This is one of the most rare and expensive pieces of Beatles sheet music issued in the United States. 8.5" x 11", $175-200.

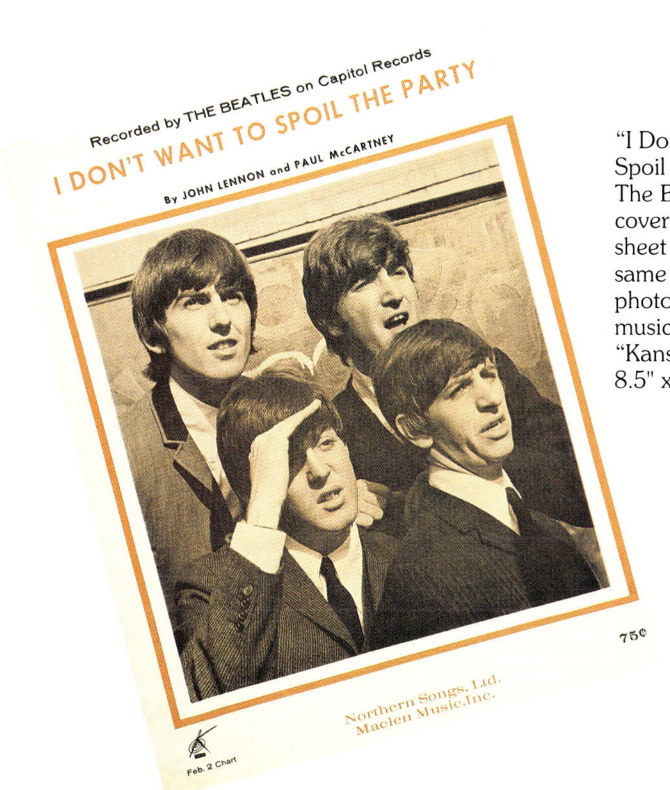


"I Don't Want To Spoil the Party" – The Beatles. The cover of this 1965 sheet shows the same "sunny day" photo that the sheet music for the song "Kansas City" uses. 8.5" x 11", $25-35.

Back cover of "Savoy Truffle."

"Day Tripper" – The Beatles. Black and white photo on a yellow background. This sheet was printed in February of 1966. 8.5" x 11", $30-40.

"Eleanor Rigby" – The Beatles. Full color cover photo showing The Beatles receiving their M.B.E. (Member of the British Empire) awards. The sheet music was printed in September of 1966. 8.5" x 11", $20-30.

"She Loves You" (France) – The Beatles. Great single color sheet from France. The title is written in French as "Elle (Il) T'Aime" or "She (He) Loves You" and the group's name is written as 'Les' Beatles. Inside, the lyrics are written in both French and English. 8.5" x 11", very rare, $25-30.

"Yesterday" – The Beatles. Extremely huge hit for The Beatles in 1965. It went to number one in the U.S. but only number eight on the British charts. The cover shows Paul's photo with an inset photo of the group. The sheet music for "Michelle" uses this same cover. 8.5" x 11", $20-35.

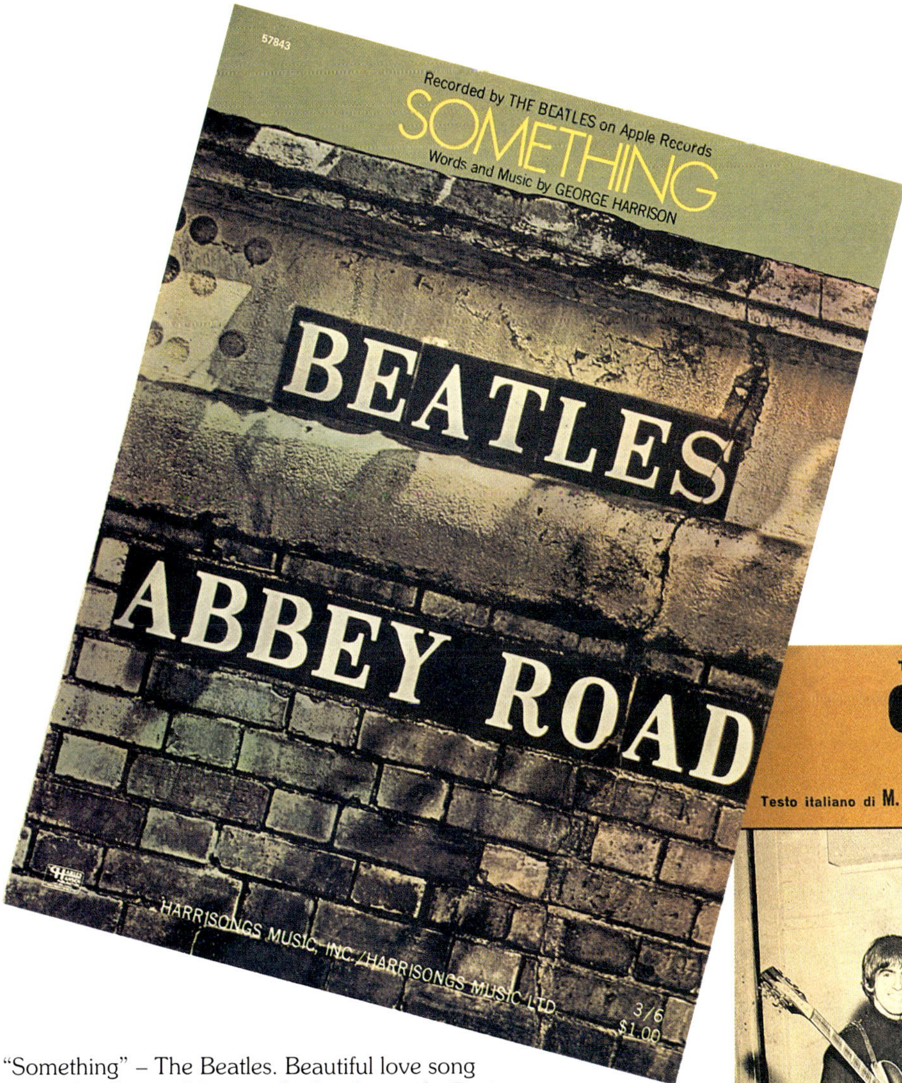


"Something" – The Beatles. Beautiful love song written by George Harrison for his then-wife, Patti Boyd. The photo from the cover of the *Abbey Road* album is shown on the back. 8.5" x 11", $15-20.

"Girl" (Italy) – The Beatles. Mini size sheet from Italy. Uncommon cover photo shows the band at a recording session—George with his Rickenbacker® guitar and Paul with his Hoffner® "Beatle" bass. Lyrics are written in both English and Italian. 6.75" x 9.75", very rare, $25-30.

Back cover of "Something," showing the Beatles famously crossing Abbey Road.

"Yellow Submarine" (U.K.) – The Beatles. Cover design created by Klaus Voorman, friend of The Beatles from Hamburg. Mr. Voorman also created the cover of the *Revolver* album. 8.5" x 11", $30-40.

"Back in The U.S.S.R." (Australia) – The Beatles. Single color sheet showing the individual photos included with *The White Album*. One-color printing was very common in Australia, where this sheet originated. 8.5" x 11", $15-20.

"Yellow Submarine" – The Beatles. Fun and colorful cartoon cover showing a tiny yellow submarine under the waves. This sheet was printed in August of 1966. 8.5" x 11", $35-45.

"No Reply" (Sweden) – The Beatles. Common photo of the band adorns this uncommon sheet from Sweden. This sheet music could have been sold within all of Scandinavia (Sweden, Norway, and Denmark) as well as Finland. However, the lyrics are written only in English. 9" x 12", very rare, $20-30.

"Ob-La-Di, Ob-La-Da" – The Beatles. Labeled as a "Deluxe Edition," this sheet music has eight pages and includes a line drawing of a man and woman on the inside cover and a montage of band photos on the page following. Printed in December of 1968. 8.5" x 11", $20-30.

"If I Fell" (U.K.) – The Beatles. This song from the album *A Hard Day's Night* shows the band in a scene from the movie of the same name. The sheet pictured here is a reproduction. 8.5" x 11", $5-10.

"Sergeant Pepper's Lonely Hearts Club Band" (Brazil) – The Beatles. This Brazilian sheet shows a black and white photo of the band for the title song from their landmark 1967 album of the same name. The lyrics are printed only in English. 9" x 12", very rare, $20-30.

"Nowhere Man" (Spain) – The Beatles. This sheet was originally authorized for sale in Spain and Portugal and shows the song title as "Sin Lugar Alguno," as well as the English translation. The lyrics that accompany the music are written in Spanish and the English lyrics are printed separately at the bottom of the third page. 8.75" x 12", very rare, $20-30.

"Ringo's Theme (This Boy)" – The Beatles. This sheet shows the standard format that was used for printing the songs from the movie *A Hard Day's Night*. This sheet was printed in August of 1964. 8.5" x 11", $35-50.

"Help" (U.K.) – The Beatles. Reproduction of the title song from The Beatles' second movie, *Help*. The same format was used on the U.S. version of this song, only with a different photo from the film. 8.5" x 11", $5-10.

"Ticket to Ride" – The Beatles. Using thick, glossy coated paper, this sheet was printed in April of 1965. The sheet music for "Day Tripper" used the same photo. 8.5" x 11", $35-50.

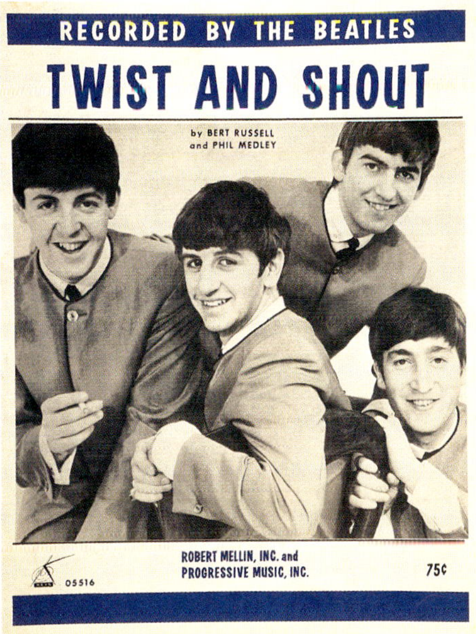


"Twist and Shout" – The Beatles. This photo and format was commonly used on U.S. sheets released in 1964; it can also be found on "Ask Me Why." 8.5" x 11", $40-60.

"Twist and Shout" (Turkey) – The Beatles. Unique mini-sheet printed in Turkey with a handwritten title. An Italian translation of the title as "Lui Non Sa" is printed on the back, along with the lyrics in both Italian and English. 7" x 9.75", very rare, $20-35.

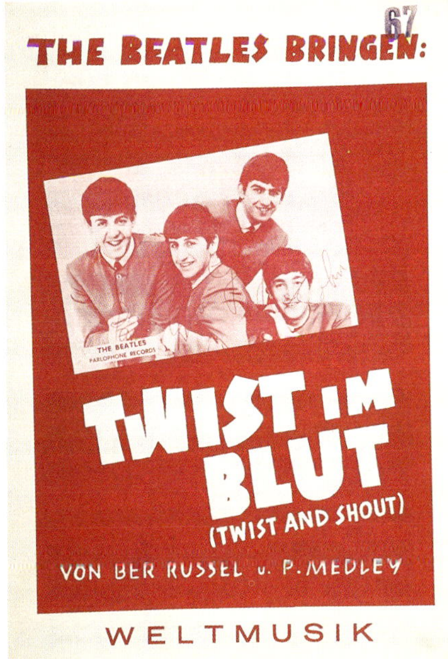


"Twist and Shout" (Germany) – The Beatles. The same photo that was used on the U.S. sheet music is also found on this German printing, but with a different layout. Copyrighted in Germany, Austria, and Switzerland. The lyrics that accompany the music are written in both German and English. 8.5" x 12", very rare, $20-35.

"The Ballad of John & Yoko" – The Beatles. A rather unhappy looking black and white picture of The Beatles with Yoko Ono. It is the only sheet that uses this photo and it is identical to the U.K. sheet for this song. 8.5" x 11", $25-35.

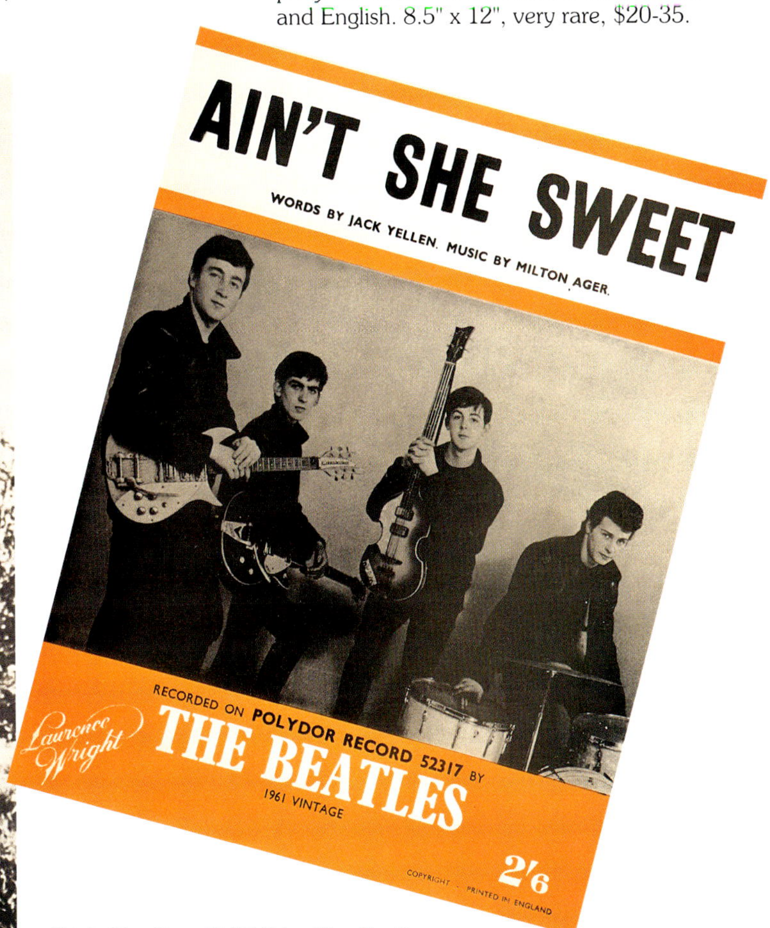


"Ain't She Sweet" (U.K.) – The Beatles. Even though this song was released in 1964, the photo on the cover is much older. It shows the group's original drummer before Ringo, Pete Best. The sheet pictured here is a reproduction. 8.5" x 11", $5-10.

## Chapter Two
# "Wipe Out"
## Surf and Folk

Surf rock began as a predominantly instrumental form of rock and roll in the early 1960s. It had a quick tempo, a lot of energy, and electronic reverb provided by the amplifiers of the day. Eventually, bands such as The Beach Boys added lyrics to the music and increased its appeal even more. It was fun music that could give the listener the feeling of the ocean and riding the surf. The sound took hold, the music took off, and it still has a strong and loyal following today.

Folk rock began back in 1965, somewhere amid The Byrds covering Bob Dylan's "Mr. Tambourine Man" and Dylan himself playing electric guitar at the Newport Folk Festival. Between those artists, and others of their kind, a new sound was created that combined the lyrics of folk with the beat of rock music. The result was a style that allowed music with a message to reach the public.

Since both styles became popular, only very specific pieces of sheet music will be considered valuable. Usually, the more desirable will be surf music, which still has a very strong fan base especially in the record collecting market.

"Pipeline" – The Chantays. Surf instrumental from southern California. Photo shows the band with their Fender® guitars. This sheet was published in April of 1963. 8.5" x 11", $30-50.

"Put a Little Love in Your Heart" – Jackie DeShannon. The cover photo of this 1969 song, which was co-written by Ms. DeShannon, shows Jackie dressed in her 60s best. 9" x 12", $10-20.

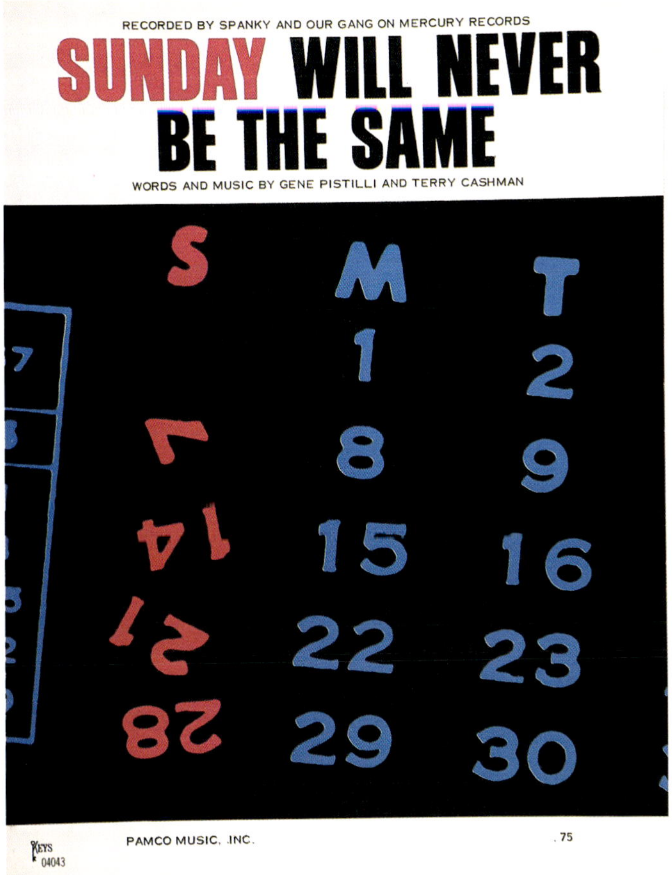


"Sunday Will Never Be the Same" – Spanky and Our Gang. Fun interpretation of the song title shows a calendar with all the Sundays mixed up—never to be the same again. 8.5" x 11", $10-15.

"Blowin' in the Wind" – Peter, Paul & Mary. This was the second of two number two hits for the group in 1963. Bob Dylan was the composer of this song. 9" x 12", $7-12.

"Leaving on a Jet Plane" – Peter, Paul & Mary. Strong, contrasting colors draw attention to the photo on this number one song written by John Denver. 9" x 12", $7-12.

"Lazy Day" – Spanky and Our Gang. Black and white cover shot of the band with fuchsia text highlights. The names of the songwriters have been cut and pasted over and around the heads of the band members. 8.5" x 11", $15-25.

"Wipe Out" (Australia) – The Surfaris. This Australian sheet markets the instrumental as "The Stomp Sensation." Unfortunately, the solid color of this 1963 sheet does little to enhance the cover photo. 8.5" x 11", $10-15.

"Wipe Out" – The Surfaris. Second of two variations of the sheet music for this song, both printed in September of 1966. No photo of the band is used, only a picture of surfers enjoying the waves. 8.5" x 11", $20-30.

"Wipe Out" – The Surfaris. This sheet is one of two U.S. versions printed to coincide with the re-release of this song in 1966. It shows photos of two surf bands that also recorded the song – The Challengers and The Ventures. The Surfaris name is misspelled as The Sufaris. 8.5" x 11", $20-40.

"Both Sides, Now" – Judy Collins. This Deluxe Edition had an original selling price of 99¢ and included a large black and white photo of Judy on the inside back cover. The cover also notes the award of Best Folk Performance to Judy Collins for her recording of this song, which was written by Joni Mitchell. 8.5" x 11", $7-12.

The Beach Boys were one of the only U.S. bands to truly challenge The Beatles with their musical creations. With Brian Wilson's songwriting and the group's perfect harmonies, they basically defined the California sound. Their sheet music is desirable, however their incredible popularity makes the sheets reasonably common, keeping the values from soaring too high for all but certain pieces.

"Mr. Dieingly Sad" – The Critters. An unusual typestyle was used for the title of this song, looking a bit like chalk on a chalkboard. Printed in September of 1966. 8.5" x 11", $20-25.

"Help Me, Rhonda" – The Beach Boys. Number one hit for the Beach Boys in 1965. The photo shows the band in their V-neck sweaters. Pictures from this session were used on a few of their sheet music covers. 9" x 12", $15-25.

"Reach Out in the Darkness" – Friend and Lover. Recorded by husband and wife team, Jim and Cathy Post. Printed in May of 1968. 8.5" x 11", $10-15.

"Then I Kissed Her" (U.K.) – The Beach Boys. The band, synonymous with surf music, recorded a song written by Phil Spector, Ellie Greenwich, and Jeff Barry. The author knows of no U.S. sheet music printed for this song. 8.5" x 11", $10-20.

"God Only Knows" (U.K. and U.S.) – The Beach Boys. The U.K. sheet shown here is particularly special, as it uses a fantastic shot of the Beach Boys from their album *Pet Sounds*. No sheet music was issued in the U.S. using this photo. The U.S. printing of "God Only Knows" shows only a standard picture of the group from a photo session. However, the back cover does show a picture of Carl Wilson, who had been designated "Beach Boy of the Month." U.K. 8.5" x 11", $35-45; U.S. 9" x 12", $15-30.

"Surfer Girl" – The Beach Boys. This is one of the more sought after Beach Boys sheets. The photos show the band frolicking in the sand and surf. David Marks, who filled in for Al Jardine for a short time, is included. Printed in August of 1963. 8.5" x 11", $40-60.

THE BEACH BOY OF THE MONTH

*CARL WILSON*, lead guitar of the Beach Boys, sings the lead on *"GOD ONLY KNOWS"*. His brother Brian, who produces all recording sessions, felt that Carl could do the best job, *for his voice range*, fit the song beautifully and because he is Brian's brother, it almost sounds like Brian.

Back cover of the U.S. version of "God Only Knows," with a nice photo of Carl Wilson. It also gives some insight into why Carl was chosen to sing lead on that song.

"Sloop John B" – The Beach Boys. One of the more colorful sheets from the Beach Boys shows the band standing on an old locomotive. Originally a traditional song, it was arranged and adapted by Brian Wilson in 1966. 9" x 12", $15-25.

"Dance, Dance, Dance" (Sweden) – The Beach Boys. The cover of this Swedish sheet shows an early photo of the group in their Pendleton shirts. The lyrics are written in English only. 8.25" x 11.5", very rare, $20-35.

"Do You Want To Dance" – The Beach Boys. This sheet was printed in April of 1965 and is considered a reprint due to the number 09999 stamped in the bottom left hand corner. 8.5" x 11", $20-40.

"The Man With All the Toys" – The Beach Boys. This photo of the Beach Boys decorating a Christmas tree was also used on the sheet music for the band's other Christmas hit, "Little Saint Nick." This sheet music is from 1964. 9" x 12", $20-50.

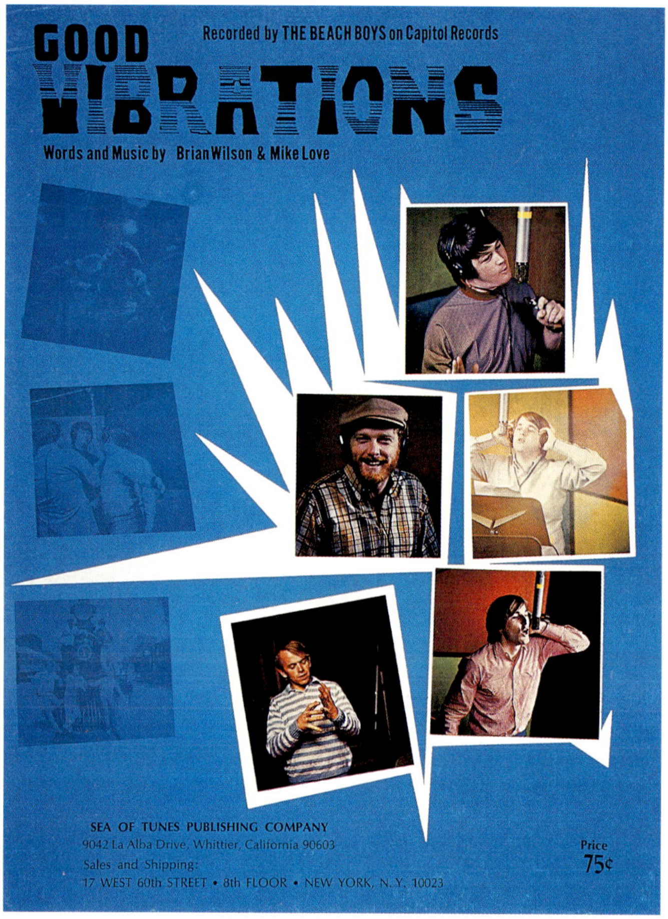

"Abraham, Martin and John" – Dion. The unique cover shows Mount Rushmore as it might have looked if our modern civil rights leaders, John Kennedy, Bobby Kennedy, and Martin Luther King, Jr., had been carved next to Abraham Lincoln. 9" x 12", $7-12.

"Good Vibrations" – The Beach Boys. The individual photos from this 1966 sheet show the Beach Boys in the recording studio. Notice the unusual typeface used for the title; it was designed to make the letters appear as if they are "vibrating." 9" x 12", $20-30.

"Midnight Confessions" – The Grass Roots. This song was the biggest hit the group had, reaching number five in 1968. It is fairly common. 8.5" x 11", $15-25.

"Let's Live for Today" – The Grass Roots. The same photo is used here as was used on "Midnight Confessions." The different colors and typestyles create completely distinct looks. Originally released in Italy with the title "Piangi Con Me," the Grass Roots version went to number eight in 1967. 8.5" x 11", $15-30.

"For What It's Worth" – The Buffalo Springfield. Stephen Stills wrote this 1967 protest song. The group was only together for a few short years, but their impact is sizeable. Sheet music from this group is rare and desirable. 9" x 12", $50-75.

"Where Were You When I Needed You" – The Grass Roots. The Grass Roots were formed after this song, written and recorded by P.F. Sloan and Steve Barri, became a minor hit in 1966. This sheet was printed in July of 1966. 8.5" x 11", $15-30.

"Eve of Destruction" – Barry McGuire. Unique and descriptive cover shows a drawing of a mushroom cloud and the letters of the title appear to be cracking at the bottom as if they are being destroyed. Also unusual is the inclusion of a photo showing the composer, P.F. Sloan. 8.5" x 11", $20-25.

"San Francisco (Be Sure To Wear Flowers in Your Hair)" – Scott McKenzie. Second, but more colorful, cover for the sheet music for this song with drawings of flowers and a picture of old San Francisco. The original shows a picture of Scott McKenzie. John Phillips of The Mamas and The Papas was the composer of this song. 8.5" x 11", $10-15.

"Like a Rolling Stone" – Bob Dylan. Initial track released from Dylan's first all electric album, *Highway 61 Revisited*. The cover uses a simple layout and a common photo. 9" x 12", $30-45.

"It Ain't Me Babe" – Bob Dylan. Early Dylan sheet with quite a young picture of Bob on the cover. The Turtles made this song popular in 1965. 9" x 12", $25-40.

"Rainy Day Women #12 & 35" – Bob Dylan. Number two hit for Dylan in 1966; kept from the top spot by another folk tune, "Monday, Monday" by The Mamas and The Papas. 9" x 12", $25-40.

"You Tell Me Why" – The Beau Brummels. Rare sheet music for San Francisco's Beau Brummels. The cover photo shows the group in matching suits and "Beatle" boots. It was printed in August of 1965. 8.5" x 11", $25-35.

"Elusive Butterfly" – Bob Lind. A simple photo of folk singer Lind was used to promote this song. The sheet was printed in April of 1966. 8.5" x 11", $10-15.

The enormously popular folk rock duo of Simon & Garfunkel started out their career under the name Tom and Jerry. A few years later, in 1965, they became an instant success with the release of "The Sounds of Silence," and subsequent releases of singles and albums solidified their status. Their sheet music is common but this is a help to the collector as no popular sheet music collection would be complete without something from this group.

"Don't Talk to Strangers" – The Beau Brummels. Another rare sheet for the Beau Brummels. The song only reached number fifty-eight in October of 1965, so just a small number of sheets were printed in November of that year. 8.5" x 11", $25-35.

"The Pied Piper" – Crispian St. Peters. Unusual color combination of purple and lime green was used to print the cover of this top ten hit. 9" x 12", $15-20.

"The Dangling Conversation" – Simon & Garfunkel. Colorized black and white photo of the duo in happy times. 8.5" x 11", $10-20.

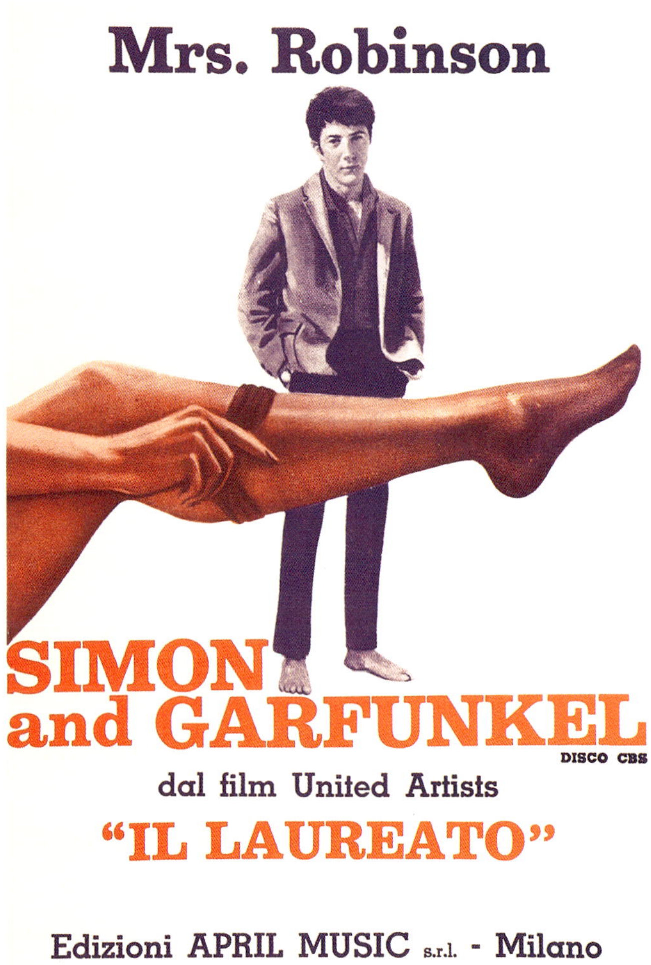


"Mrs. Robinson" (Italy) – Simon & Garfunkel. Italian mini-sheet uses a photo of Anne Bancroft's leg and a confused Dustin Hoffman for this song from the movie "Il Laureato" (*The Graduate*). The U.S. version is not nearly as interesting, as it contains only a line drawing on a fuchsia background. 6.75" x 9.75", very rare, $15-30.

"Homeward Bound" (U.K.) – Simon & Garfunkel. Paul Simon's poignant tale of life on tour. This sheet appears to be a later printing due to the £20p (20 pence) original selling price. Sheets actually printed in 1966 would normally have a price of £3/- or three shillings. 8.5" x 11", $10-20.

"I Am a Rock" – Simon & Garfunkel. Pensive, cigarette smoking solo shots, along with a group shot taken the same day, are used on this July 1966 sheet. 8.5" x 11", $10-15.

"Sounds of Silence" – Simon & Garfunkel. The cover seen on this February 1966 sheet is common and was used on sheet music for other bands as well. 8.5" x 11", $10-15.

"Bridge Over Troubled Water" – Simon & Garfunkel. Very common printing of the hit song with a grainy, full-color photo of the duo. 9" x 12", $10-15.

Playful photo from the back cover of "Bridge Over Troubled Water."

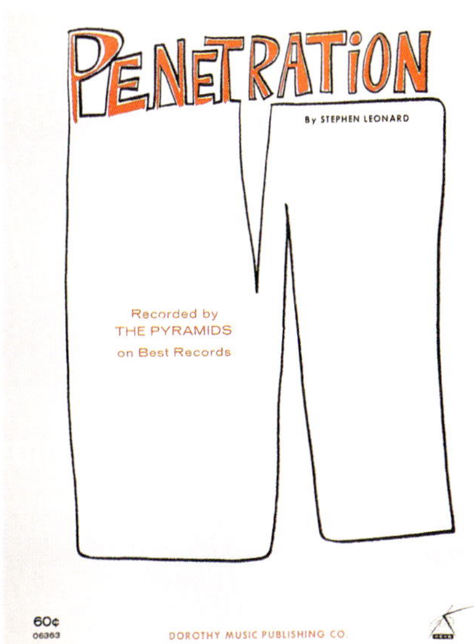


"Penetration" – The Pyramids. Simple, hand drawn cover art is a nice accompaniment to this instrumental. Printed in February of 1964 with an original selling price of 60¢. 8.5" x 11", $10-15.

"You Were on My Mind" – We Five. In a peculiar attempt to illustrate the band's name, an array of numbers is used to frame the cover photo. Sylvia Fricker of Ian and Sylvia wrote this song. 9" x 12", $15-25.

"Honolulu Lulu" – Jan and Dean. Standard cover layout that was used on sheet music printings for other bands. The same photo that is used on this sheet was used on "Surf City." 8.5" x 11", $30-50.

"Surf City" – Jan and Dean. Consummate surf song shows the duo with their boards at the beach and was printed in June of 1963. Written by Brian Wilson of The Beach Boys and Jan Berry. 8.5" x 11", $35-55.

"You Really Know How To Hurt a Guy" – Jan and Dean. Truly bizarre photos show the duo visiting [Madame] Tussaud's Hollywood Wax Museum in California. Printed in May of 1965. 8.5" x 11", $15-25.

"Mr. Tambourine Man" – The Byrds. One of the first truly successful marriages of folk and rock; it was part of the beginning of the folk-rock movement in music in 1965. Written by Bob Dylan. 9" x 12", $30-40.

"Turn! Turn! Turn!" – The Byrds. Taken from the Book of Ecclesiastes and adapted by Pete Seger, this tune became a chart topper for The Byrds in 1965. Cover shows the same photo from their album *Mr. Tambourine Man*, even though this song was not included with that record. 9" x 12", $30-40.

"California Dreamin'" – The Mamas and The Papas. Appropriately dreamy photo of the group conveys the feeling of the song. Printed in March of 1966. 8.5" x 11", $20-30.

"Telstar" (U.K.) – The Tornados. This song took its name from the very first communications satellite, which is pictured on the cover. The British band took the song all the way to number one in both the United States and Britain. 8.5" x 11", $15-30.

"My Back Pages" – The Byrds. Rare 1967 sheet that pictures the group as a quartet after Gene Clark had left the band. Written by Bob Dylan. 9" x 12", $40-55.

"Creeque Alley" (U.S. and U.K.) – The Mamas and The Papas. These two pieces together are a great example of the differences between U.S. and U.K. sheet music. The U.S. sheet shows a wonderfully fun-loving, full color picture of the group cavorting in the water. It epitomizes the look of U.S. sheet music of the time. The U.K. sheet shows quite a different cover treatment than that of the U.S.; it is a basic layout used for sheet music printed in the U.K. during the 1960s. Both 8.5" x 11", U.S. $20-35; U.K. $15-20.

"Monday, Monday" – The Mamas and The Papas. Only number one hit for the group. This song is still heard on the radio and enjoyed today. The sheet was printed in May of 1966. 8.5" x 11", $25-35

"Dedicated to the One I Love" – The Mamas and The Papas. Picture for this cover was taken during the same session as the one for the cover of "Creeque Alley." The name of the group is written in tiny, hot pink letters above John Phillips' head. 8.5" x 11", $20-25.

"Words of Love" – The Mamas and The Papas. The band is almost lost in the grass in this casual photo. Written by John Phillips and sung by Cass Elliott, this song hit the top ten in 1966. 8.5" x 11", $15-25.

"I Saw Her Again Last Night" – The Mamas and The Papas. This song was written in response to Denny Doherty's affair with Michelle Phillips, wife of John. 8.5" x 11", $15-25.

"Get Together" – The Young Bloods. Written in 1963, recorded in 1967, and reached number five in 1969. The band's name is shown as two words on the cover of the sheet music, even though all their albums show the name as one word. 9" x 12", $10-15.

"Daydream" – The Lovin' Spoonful. Comical photo of the band during a "hunting" trip having caught fur-clad John Sebastian as the quarry. 9" x 12", $15-20.

"Do You Believe in Magic?" – The Lovin' Spoonful. Title song from the Spoonful's first album in 1965. 9" x 12", $15-20.

"Nashville Cats" – The Lovin' Spoonful. Great high angle shot of the band; the sheet music is from 1966. 9" x 12", $15-20.

The Lovin' Spoonful started out playing in small clubs in New York and ended up one of the top groups of the Sixties. They combined many different styles of music, including folk, jug band, and straightforward rock and roll into a unique "good time" sound. Their sheet music is as special as the music itself with no two pieces having similar photos or styles.

"Did You Ever Have To Make Up Your Mind?" – The Lovin' Spoonful. A song about tough decisions. The title is enclosed in a callout balloon leading from the song's composer, John Sebastian. 9" x 12", $15-20.

"Summer in the City" – The Lovin' Spoonful. Descriptive cover showing not only a band photo but also a drawing of kids playing in the water of an open hydrant on a city street. 9" x 12", $15-25.

"In the Year 2525 (Exordium & Terminus)" (Australia) – Zager & Evans. Bleak view of the future as written by half of the duo that recorded it, Rick Evans. The cover of this 1969 Australian printing is virtually identical to the U.S. version. 8.5" x 11", $10-20.

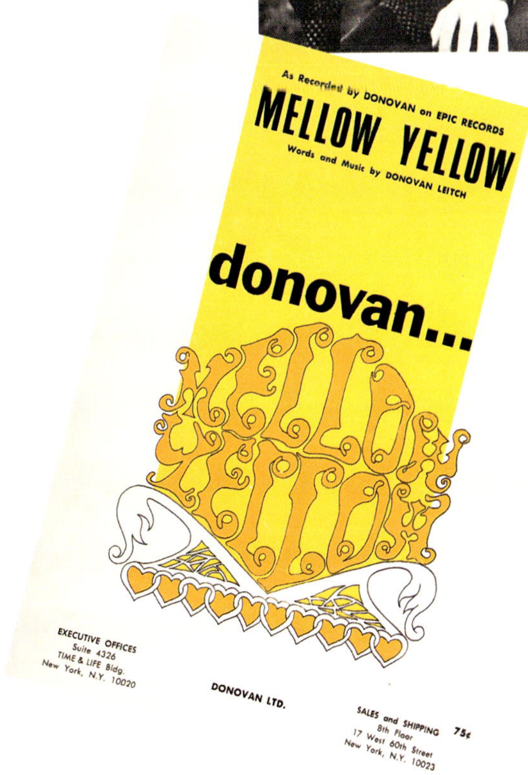


"Mellow Yellow" – Donovan. Appropriately yellow cover of this 1966 sheet music has the song title written in such a psychedelic fashion that the letters are almost illegible. Some printings of this song have a full yellow cover, rather than yellow and white. 9" x 12", $20-30.

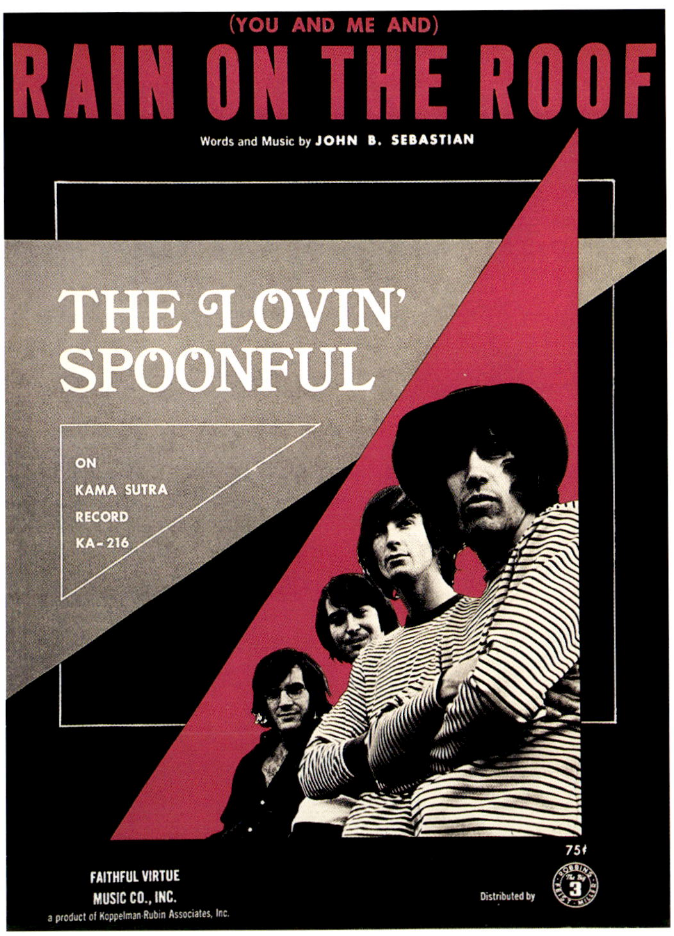


"(You and Me and) Rain on the Roof" – The Lovin' Spoonful. While commonly known as "Rain on the Roof," the 1966 sheet music uses a longer title. 9" x 12", $15-20.

"Sunshine Superman" – Donovan. This number one song from 1966 blends an interesting combination of folk-rock and psychedelia. 9" x 12", $20-30.

"Cinderella-Rockefella" (U.K.) – Ester and Abi Ofarim. Husband and wife duo from Israel dressed in their 1960s finery. 8.5" x 11", $7-12.

"Georgy Girl" (U.K.) – The Seekers. Title song from the movie of the same name. This U.K. printing is quite special since it shows individual photos of each member of the group. The U.S. sheet music is not nearly as attractive, showing "floating head" shots of actors from the movie. 8.5" x 11", $10-15.

"I'll Never Find Another You" – The Seekers. Simple cover in shades of blue. Tom Springfield from the group The Springfields (and brother of soul singer, Dusty) wrote this song. 9" x 12", $10-15.

"Walk, Don't Run '64" – The Ventures. Surf bands were often pictured with their instruments, and the cover of this 1964 sheet is no exception. It shows the band with the Ventures' signature model of the Mosrite® guitar. Printed in August of 1964. 8.5" x 11", $50-75.

"Hawaii Five-O" – The Ventures. Theme song to the long-running TV crime drama that began in 1968. The original selling price was only 85¢. 9" x 12", $20-30.

# Chapter Three
# "Psychotic Reaction"
## Garage, Hard Rock, and Psychedelia

With its pounding beat, hard rock sounded like rock and roll on overdrive. It became more popular by the second half of the decade, earning many loyal fans. These fans have made sheet music from hard rock artists very desirable. While usually uncommon, pieces will come up for sale once or twice a year.

Garage rock, with its simple, raw, and occasionally amateurish sound, and psychedelic music, which used distorted effects and fluid melodies, can have quite different followings than hard rock. While there were a number of groups that had hits, most did not, soon fading into obscurity. This obscurity caused little (if any) sheet music to be printed for their songs, which makes it quite rare and very difficult to obtain—but not necessarily more valuable.

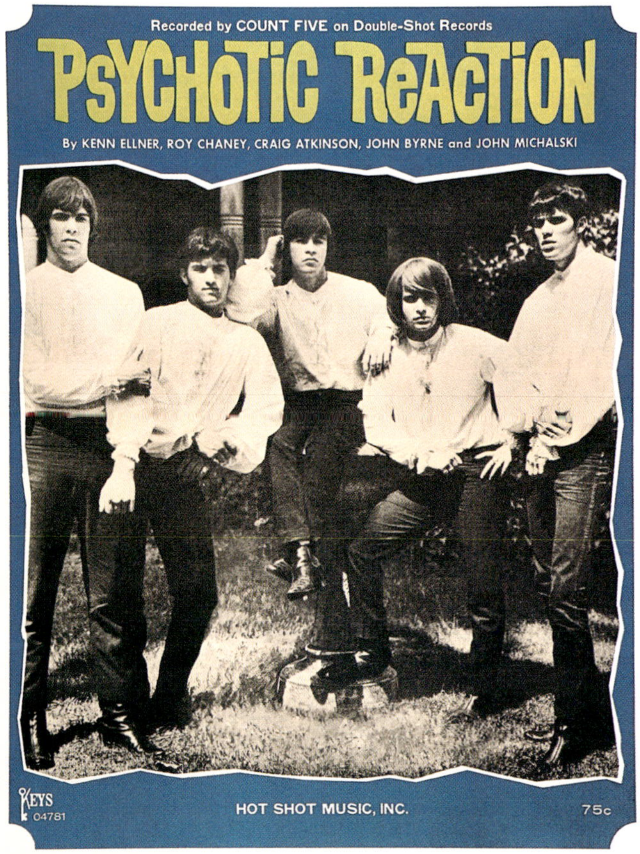


"Psychotic Reaction" – Count Five. This garage-rock classic was written by the band themselves. Printed in October of 1966. 8.5" x 11", $20-35.

"Somebody To Love" – The Jefferson Airplane. First hit for this San Francisco based band. The same cover is used on the sheet music for "White Rabbit," only with different colors. 9" x 12", $30-45.

"In-A-Gadda-Da-Vida" – Iron Butterfly. 1969 printing of the 17 minute opus from 1968. The original title was supposed to be "In the Garden of Eden" but the band was apparently too inebriated to pronounce it properly and it was renamed. 9" x 12", $15-30.

"Dirty Water" – The Standells. This song about Boston and the water of the River Charles caused many casual listeners to assume the band was from that city as well. They weren't—they were from Los Angeles. 8.5" x 11", $20-35.

"Sometimes Good Guys Don't Wear White" – The Standells. Cover features a really nice shot of the band performing in 1966. 8.5" x 11", $20-40.

"I Could Be So Good to You" – Don and The Goodtimes. This band from the Pacific Northwest was only able to take this song about halfway to the top in April of 1967. 9" x 12", $15-30.

"Louie, Louie" – The Kingsmen. Quintessential song from the 1960s garage-rock era. Very simple cover mentions that it was also recorded by Richard Berry, the composer, as well as Paul Revere and The Raiders. The original selling price is actually "60 cents," not 75¢ as the price sticker indicates. 9" x 12", $30-45.

"Killer Joe" – The Kingsmen. This song didn't chart too high when it was released in 1966, but this "killer" photo of the band in concert almost makes up for it. 8.5" x 11", $25-40.

"My Wife Can't Cook" – The Kingsmen. Unusually common sheet music for a song that really didn't do well at the time of its original release. 9" x 12", $15-20.

"A House in the Country" (U.K.) – The Pretty Things. Desirable piece of sheet music that has sold for as much as $70 at auction. Written by Ray Davies of The Kinks. 8.5" x 11", $40-50.

"Journey to the Center of the Mind" – The Amboy Dukes. Co-written by guitar legend Ted Nugent, who was also a member of the band. Note the ultra psychedelic wardrobe worn in the photo. Value 8.5" x 11", $20-35.

Close up photo of Ted Nugent from his time with The Amboy Dukes.

"She's About a Mover" – Sir Douglas Quintet. This band from Texas named themselves with a decidedly English sounding moniker to compete with the British Invasion. 8.5" x 11", $10-15.

"Don't Worry Mother (Your Son's Heart Is Pure)" – The McCoys. Uncommon sheet showing the band posed with their guitars. 8.5" x 11", $20-30.

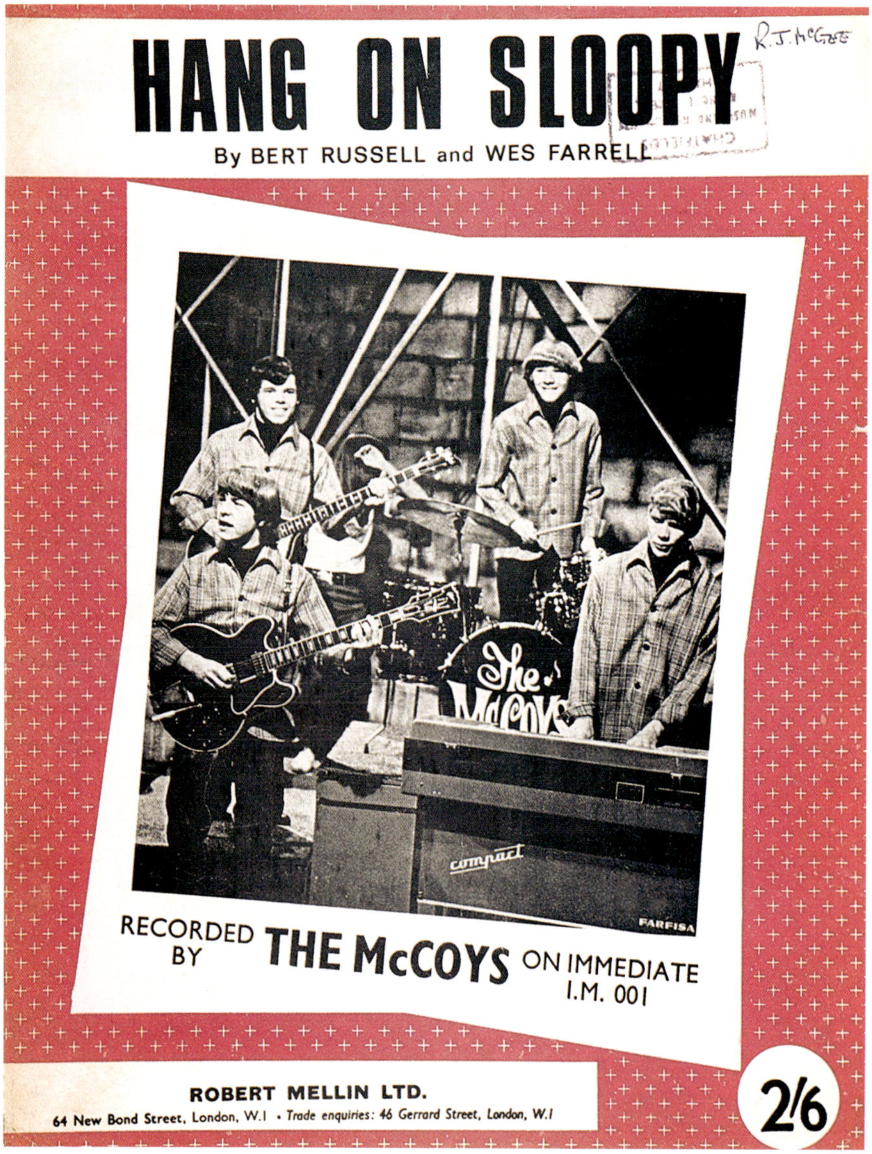


"Hang On Sloopy" (U.K.) – The McCoys. Unique performance shot of the band with clearly visible Gibson® guitar and Farfisa® organ… not to mention those matching jackets! No band picture was shown on the U.S. printing. 8.5" x 11", $20-35.

"(Hang On Sloopy) My Girl Sloopy" – The McCoys. The sheet music for this garage classic and number one hit for The McCoys does not show a picture of the band or mention their name. It does, however, show the original title for the song, "My Girl Sloopy." It was changed by band guitarist Rick Zheringer (later Derringer), since that particular phrase is never heard in the song itself. 8.5" x 11", $10-15.

"Hey Joe" – The Leaves. Same song recorded and made famous by Jimi Hendrix, but with a completely different (and up tempo) beat. 9" x 12", $20-40.

"All Along the Watchtower" – The Jimi Hendrix Experience. The fluid typestyle of the band name and the op-art design of the background give the cover of this sheet a decidedly psychedelic feeling. The song was written by Bob Dylan. 9" x 12", $40-60.

During their most popular years, 1965-1967, the record sales of Paul Revere & The Raiders rivaled that of The Beatles. This was helped in no small part by their appearance on the daily television show *Where The Action Is*. Their high-energy performances and charismatic lead singer, Mark Lindsay, made them the darlings of many a young teenage girl, even though history books largely pass over them.

"Hungry" – Paul Revere and The Raiders. Second or possibly third printing of the sheet music for this song. An earlier printing shows the same cover, only in orange instead of blue. There is no difference in value. 8.5" x 11", $20-35.

"Good Thing" – Paul Revere and The Raiders. Nice color photo of the band in their Revolutionary War uniforms. This sheet was printed in January of 1967. 8.5" x 11", $20-25.

"The Great Airplane Strike" – Paul Revere and The Raiders. The two sheets shown here are for the same song and were both printed in the same month, October 1966. The group had changed guitarists a few months before the release of this song, but the color sheet (which shows the year in the song title) was accidentally produced still showing original guitarist Drake Levin (behind the pole). When the error was noticed, the corrected cover showing new guitar player Jim "Harpo" Valley was printed in black and white. Both 8.5" x 11", Color $25-35; B&W $20-30.

"Him or Me, What's It Gonna Be" – Paul Revere and The Raiders. Outstanding, bright red cover highlights the studio shot of the group. The band changed members on a few occasions and this is the last sheet music printed (May 1967) with this line up. 8.5" x 11", $25-35.

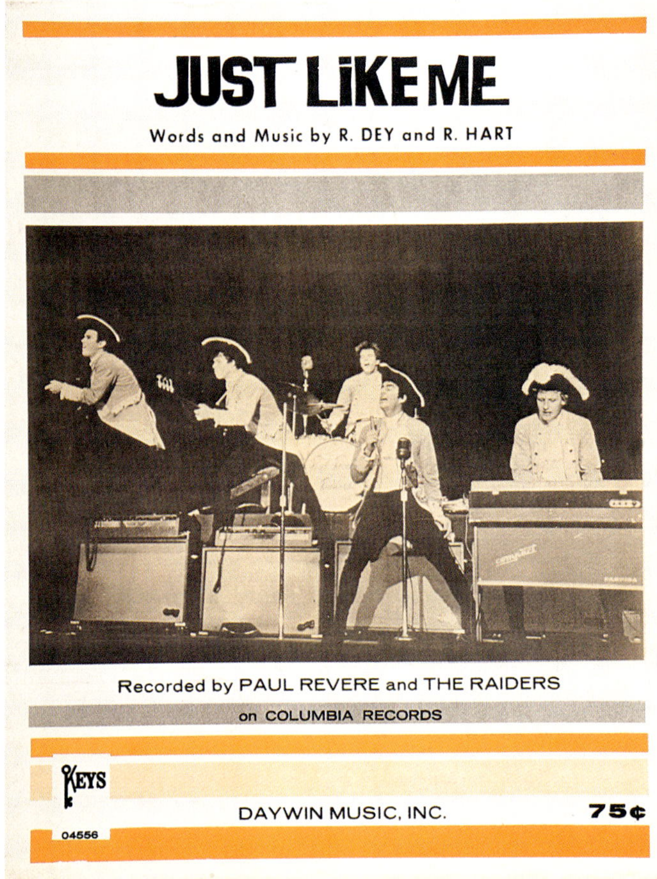


"Just Like Me" – Paul Revere and The Raiders. Live shot of the band performing was used on the cover. The photo shows keyboardist Paul Revere with his Farfisa® organ. The same photo was used on the "Steppin' Out" sheet. 8.5" x 11", $25-30.

"Little Girl" (Italy) – Paul Revere and The Raiders. Mini-sheet printed in Italy with great American imagery on the cover. The original title of the song is "Little Girl In the 4th Row." The lyrics are printed in both Italian and English on the inside. 6.75" x 9.75", very rare, $20-30.

"Kicks" – Paul Revere and The Raiders. Since this song was quite a big hit for the band, there were numerous printings of the sheet music. Two printings in shades of pink and one in a light blue are known. There is no difference in value. 8.5" x 11", $20-30.

"Piece Of My Heart" – Janis Joplin and Big Brother & The Holding Company. The gentle, solid color printing of this sheet belies the emotion and power of this track. Janis went solo a few months after its release. 8.5" x 11", $20-40.

"Steppin' Out" – Paul Revere and The Raiders. Early and uncommon sheet showing the band in concert. The same photo was used on the sheet music for "Just Like Me." This sheet was printed in November of 1965. 8.5" x 11", $25-40.

"Me and Bobby McGee" – Janis Joplin. This song became a hit for Janis in 1971. 8.5" x 11", $20-35.

"Like Longhair" – Paul Revere and The Raiders. First printing (April 1961) of the sheet music for this instrumental. The cover shows an original selling price of 60¢, while later printings show the same cover with a price of 75¢. 9" x 12", $25-35.

"Black" (Australia) – The Throb. Short-lived Australian garage-punk band. While the cover shows only two band members and the title, the sheet opens to show a full frame photo of the band performing live that wraps around to the back. Pictured here, fully open, showing both front and back covers. 8.5" x 11", rare, $30-45.

"Run, Run, Run" – The Third Rail. Half sung and half spoken tune about life as part of the rat race. Very common cover style used with many bands and songs. This particular sheet was printed in August of 1967. 8.5" x 11", $10-15.

"96 Tears" – ? and The Mysterians. The real name of ? (Question Mark) is revealed here as he, also known as Rudy Martinez, is identified as writing both the words and music to this hit. 8.5" x 11", $15-30.

"A Whiter Shade of Pale" – Procol Harum. One of the least lyrically understood songs of the decade. This is a second printing of the sheet music; the first shows a close-up photo of the band. 9" x 12", $20-25.

"Gloria" – Shadows Of Knight. Top ten hit for this Chicago based band; written by Van Morrison. 9" x 12", $20-35.

"Blackberry Way" (Australia) – The Move. Great photo of the band showing late 1960s clothing and hairstyles. The same photo was used for both this and the U.K. printing. No sheet music was printed for this song in the United States. 8.5" x 11", $20-25.

"Shake" – Shadows Of Knight. Very simple cover for this 1968 sheet, made interesting by the typestyle used for the song title. Notice how the extra lines and uneven letters make the words appear to move or "shake." 9" x 12", $15-25.

"Green Tambourine" – The Lemon Pipers. Extremely descriptive cover drawing of, what else—a green tambourine. This sheet music was printed in April of 1968. 8.5" x 11", $15-25.

"Bend Me, Shape Me" – The American Breed. This second single for the band hit the top five. Since this song was released in 1967 (notice the Nehru jackets on the two center figures), the original selling price is actually only 75¢ not $1.95, which is shown by a sticker covering the price on this particular sheet. 9" x 12", $20-35.

"Jelly Jungle (Of Orange Marmalade)" – The Lemon Pipers. Super-sweet title with lyrics that are even sweeter. Since the song mentions the color orange, that's the color used to print the sheet music. 9" x 12", $15-20.

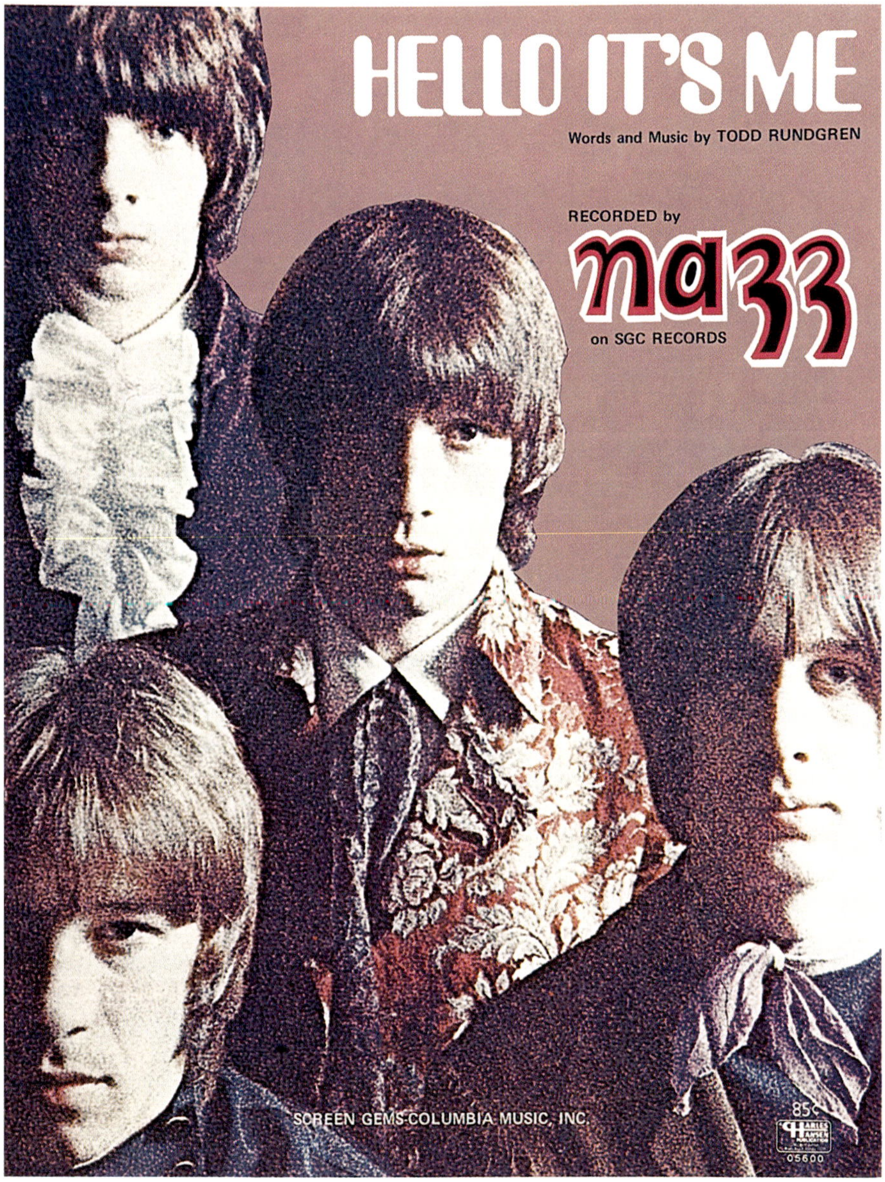


"Hello It's Me" – Nazz. Nazz was an American band paying homage to the British Invasion with their manor of dress (as evidenced in this cover photo) and music; this 1969 song was a low charting hit. Todd Rundgren, who wrote this song, recorded it as a solo artist a few years later with greater success. 8.5" x 11", $40-60.

Stylish ruffians, The Who paved the way for many a hard rock act with their stage antics, which included explosions and smashed guitars. Although their style has never quite been duplicated, their musical influence is immeasurable. U.S. sheet music for The Who's early songs is very difficult to find, if it exists at all, since they didn't really have success here until after the 1967 Monterey Pop Festival. Buyers must turn to U.K. printings in order to collect important songs from this band's early years.

"I'm a Boy" (U.K.) – The Who. Animated photo of the band joking around with a skateboard. Sheet music was not printed for this song in the United States. 8.5" x 11", $45-60.

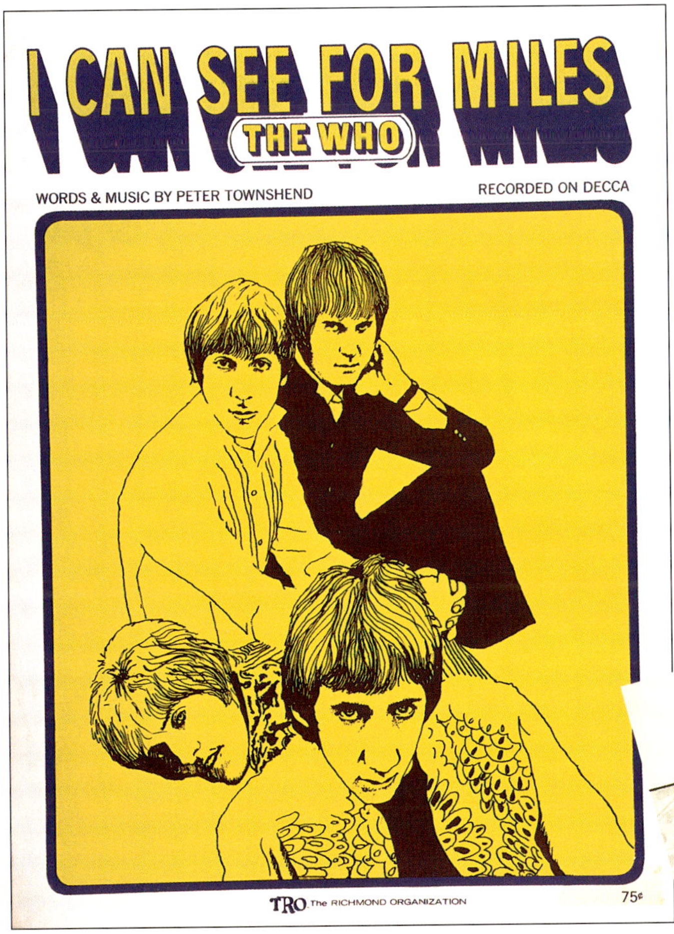


"I Can See For Miles" – The Who. Line drawing of the band graces this lime green and purple cover. Inside, the music and lyrics are also printed in purple, which is unusual as most music is printed in black no matter what color is on the cover. 9" x 12", $30-45.

"My Generation" (U.K.) – The Who. A 1966 song that epitomizes rebellious youth and teen angst. In a rebellious statement of his own, Pete Townshend is photographed wearing his country's flag as a coat. 8.5" x 11", $50-65.

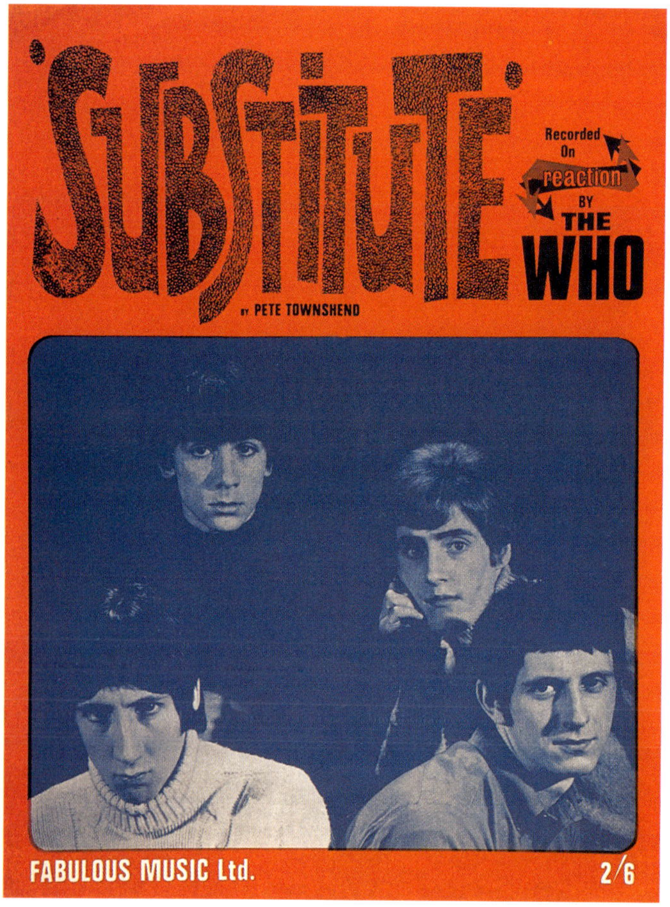


"Substitute" (U.K.) – The Who. The red and blue cover on this 1966 sheet shows an appropriately moody photo of the band. 8.5" x 11", $35-50.

"Pictures of Lily" (U.K.) – The Who. Burlesque photos adorn the cover of this 1967 song. The Australian version uses the same cover only with the words printed in yellow, making that version a bit more desirable than the U.K. version, which is unusual. 8.5" x 11", $30-45.

"Overture (From Tommy)" – The Who. Full color photo of the band in their late 1960s leather and fringe finery. This is an instrumental track from the rock-opera *Tommy*. 8.5" x 11", $25-35.

"Magic Bus" (U.K.) – The Who. 1968 release from the album of the same name. Photo placed in the windshield makes it appear as if the band is actually riding the bus. Song title, band name, and bus are all hand drawn and convey the "magical" feeling of the song. 8.5" x 11", $40-45.

"I Can't Explain" (U.K.) – The Who. First single for The Who in both the United States and the United Kingdom. The sheet is printed in the standard fashion that most U.K. sheets were printed in at the time. Since this was the band's first release, no extra time or creativity was expended, unlike with later sheet music printings. 8.5" x 11", $45-60.

"San Francisco Girls" – Fever Tree. Low charting psychedelic song from this Houston band. 8.5" x 11", $10-15.

"Sunshine of Your Love" – Cream. First printing of this hard rock hit from June 1968. The second printing (August 1968) has a completely different photo and is yellow and black. 8.5" x 11", $20-35.

"Up on the Roof" – The Cryan' Shames. This is the same song that was recorded by The Drifters in 1963. The sheet music for this version was printed in 1968. 8.5" x 11", $25-30.

"White Room" – Cream. Co-written by vocalist/bassist Jack Bruce with Eric Clapton on guitar. Printed in October of 1968. 8.5" x 11", $20-35.

Back cover of the "7 and 7 Is" sheet music at right, showing how to contact the band's fan club called The Love Society. You could become a member for all of $2.00.

"7 and 7 Is" – Love. One of the greatest sheet music covers of the 1960s. The bright colors and psychedelic style completely convey the mood of the song and the feeling of the decade. 8.5" x 11", $40-60.

"Spread It On Thick" – The Gentrys. The Gentrys featured Jimmy Hart as one of the vocalists. Hart went on to become a manager in professional wrestling and was known as "The Mouth of the South." This sheet music was printed in January of 1966. 8.5" x 11", $15-25.

"Keep On Dancing" – The Gentrys. This song was the biggest hit for the band, but it was originally too short for radio play so a section of the music was added on to the end. Just when the listener thinks the song is going to finish, there is a break and it begins again. This song became a hit for the band in 1965. 9" x 12", $25-40.

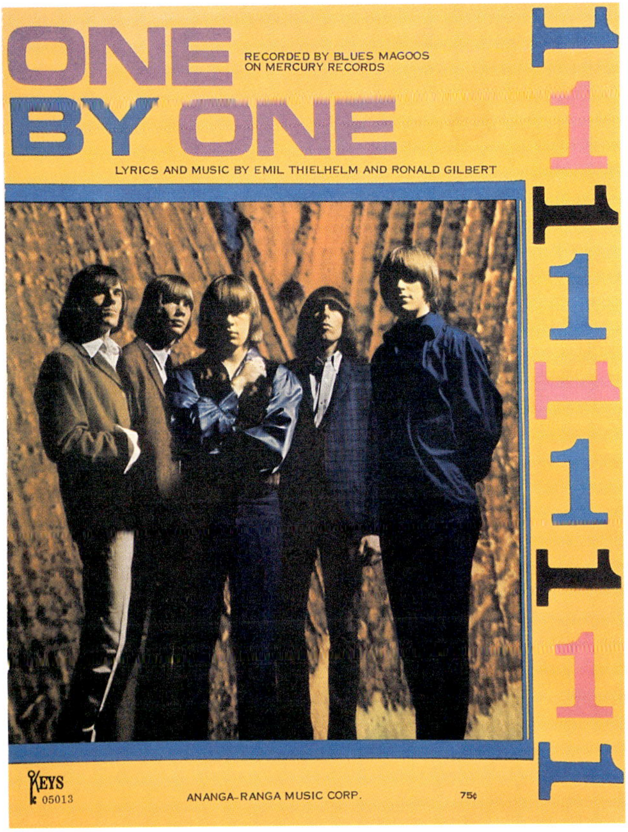


"One By One" – The Blues Magoos. Another descriptive cover, showing colorful number 1s down the side. Printed in June of 1967. 8.5" x 11", $20-30.

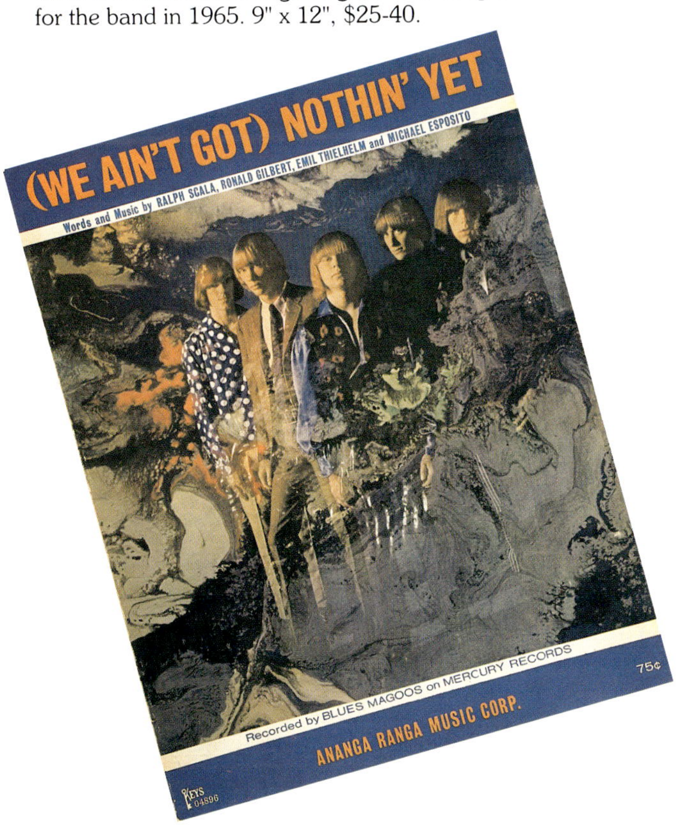


"(We Ain't Got) Nothin' Yet" – The Blues Magoos. A truly psychedelic piece of sheet music if there ever was one! Swirly colors are superimposed over a band photo, giving this sheet a look unlike any other. Printed in January of 1967. 8.5" x 11", $20-35.

"There's a Chance We Can Make It" – The Blues Magoos. Printed in April of 1967. The 45rpm was released with "Pipe Dream" on the flip side. 8.5" x 11", $20-30.

"Pipe Dream" – The Blues Magoos. Printed in April of 1967 with the band photo surrounded by an actual drawing of a pipe. 8.5" x 11", $20-30.

"Moulty" – The Barbarians. Mostly spoken word, slightly autobiographical tune about the band's drummer, Victor Moulton. Moulton had only one hand and wore a hook, as can been seen in the photo. 8.5" x 11", $20-40.

"Little Bit O' Soul" – The Music Explosion. Common cover that can be found on other sheet music for different bands and songs. 9" x 12", $20-25.

"Are You a Boy or Are You a Girl" – The Barbarians. Studio shot of the band in their matching shirts and sandals. The song is about the type of questions that arose when faced with men wearing the fashionable long hair of the day. 8.5" x 11", $20-40.

"That Acapulco Gold" – The Rainy Daze. The cover shows a fairly uptight looking photo for the psychedelic quintet from Denver. The back cover contains more casual photos of the band. 9" x 12", $15-25.

Back cover of "That Acapulco Gold." It shows four photos of the band, including one of them performing, and bios of each band member.

The California-based band The Doors became one of the seminal hard rock groups of the 1960s. Their music was a melding of many influences, giving them a unique style and a lasting musical presence. Doors sheet music is very interesting in its simplicity. All but one of their sheet music releases was printed in black and white. Each one is quite different from the other, but no color was used except on "Light My Fire."

"Hello I Love You, Won't You Tell Me Your Name" – The Doors. Generally known by the shortened title of "Hello, I Love You" this song was a number one hit for The Doors in 1968. 9" x 12", $25-35.

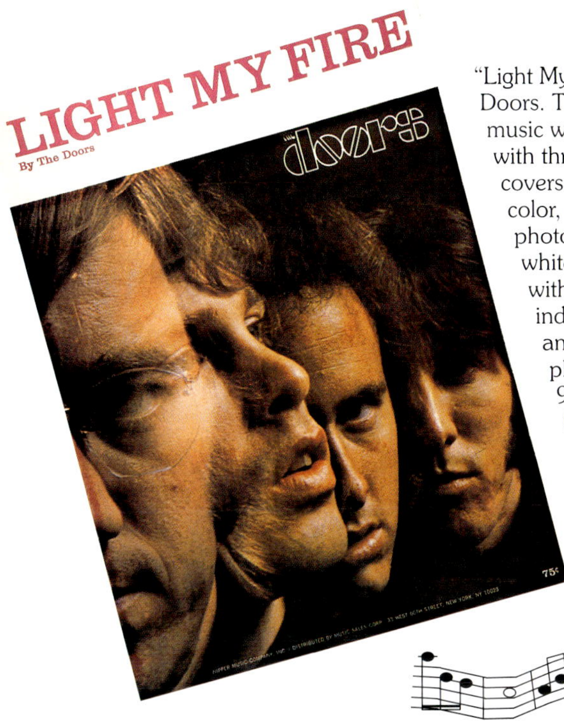


"Light My Fire" – The Doors. This sheet music was released with three different covers. This one in color, the same photo in black and white, and the last with four individual black and white photos. 9" x 12", $30-35.

"Love Me Two Times" – The Doors. Interesting overhead shot of the band, as usual, in black and white. 9" x 12", $20-35.

"Touch Me" (U.K. and U.S.) – The Doors. The U.K. sheet uses a cover that is a standard style from the time while the U.S. release uses a more unusual cover style. The same photo is used on both sheets but the images have been rearranged on the one from the United States. U.K. 8.5" x 11", $15-30; U.S. 9" x 12", $20-35.

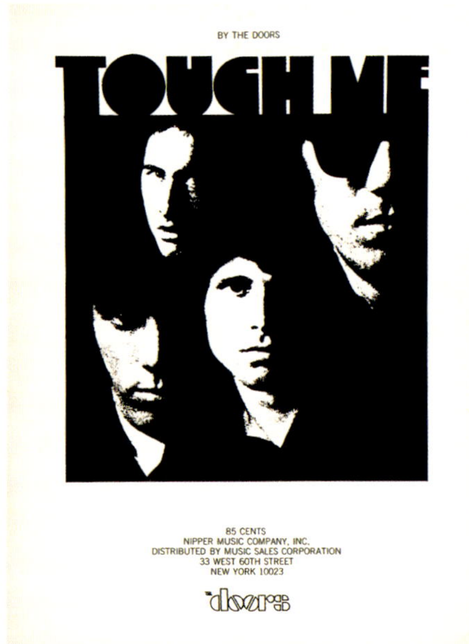

"Incense and Peppermints" – The Strawberry Alarm Clock. Title track from their debut album uses the same photo that was used on the album cover. 9" x 12", $20-25.

"You Keep Me Hangin' On" – Vanilla Fudge. Written by the Motown songwriting team of Holland, Dozier and Holland and previously recorded by The Supremes. This sheet music most likely dates from 1968, since this version of the song was released twice (1967 and 1968), with the second release charting much higher. 9" x 12", $20-30.

"Sunshine Cottage" – The Herd. British group featuring guitarist Peter Frampton, who co-wrote this song. 8.5" x 11", $10-15.

"I Want Candy" – The Strangeloves. The Strangeloves were a trio of men from Brooklyn, New York, but they created a new identity for their group and claimed they were from the Australian outback, hence the drums and spears in their photographs. This is the same song that was recorded by Bow Wow Wow in the early 1980s. 8.5" x 11", $25-30.

"Night Time" – The Strangeloves. Band members Bob Feldman, Jerry Goldstein, and Richard Gottehrer, who wrote this song for their group, also wrote "My Boyfriend's Back," which was a number one hit for The Angels in 1963. 8.5" x 11", $20-25.

"Nobody But Me" – The Human Beinz. Originally written and recorded by the Isley Brothers in 1962, this song became a top ten hit for The Human Beinz in 1967. 8.5" x 11", $20-35.

"The Shape Of Things To Come" – Max Frost and The Troopers. From the 1968 movie *Wild In the Streets*. The band was only a studio group, which existed solely for the purpose of recording music for the movie. 8.5" x 11", $15-25.

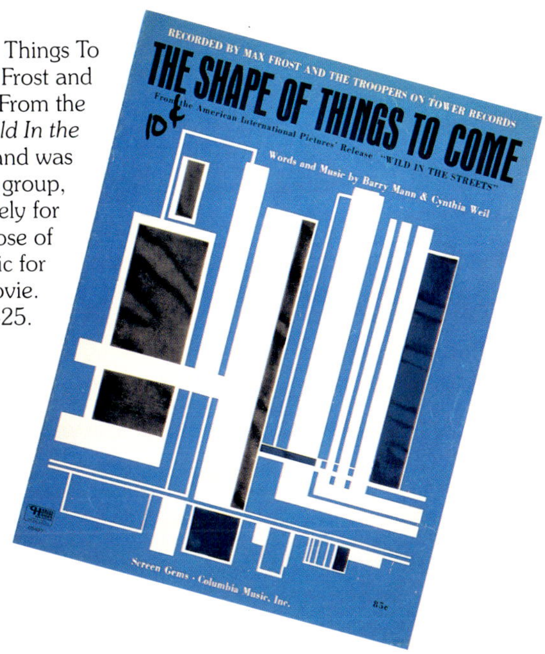

"Time Won't Let Me" – The Outsiders. Number five hit for The Outsiders in 1966. This is the second sheet music printing for this song from May of 1966. 8.5" x 11", $15-30.

"Respectable" – The Outsiders. Written by The Isley Brothers, The Outsiders took this song to number fifteen in 1966. 8.5" x 11", $15-20.

"Time Won't Let Me" – The Outsiders. This first printing mentions the name of the group but does not show their picture. Sheet printed in April of 1966. 8.5" x 11", $10-15.

"Pushin' Too Hard" – The Seeds. Written by Sky Saxon, vocalist and bass player for the group. "Pushin' Too Hard" was the first single for the band. 9" x 12", $20-30.

"Girl In Love" – The Outsiders. Uncommon sheet for The Outsiders printed in June of 1966. 8.5" x 11", $15-20.

"Lies (Are Breakin' My Heart)" – The Knickerbockers. Second printing of sheet music for this song. The other had the same cover, only in full color. This sheet was printed in March of 1966. 8.5" x 11", $20-30.

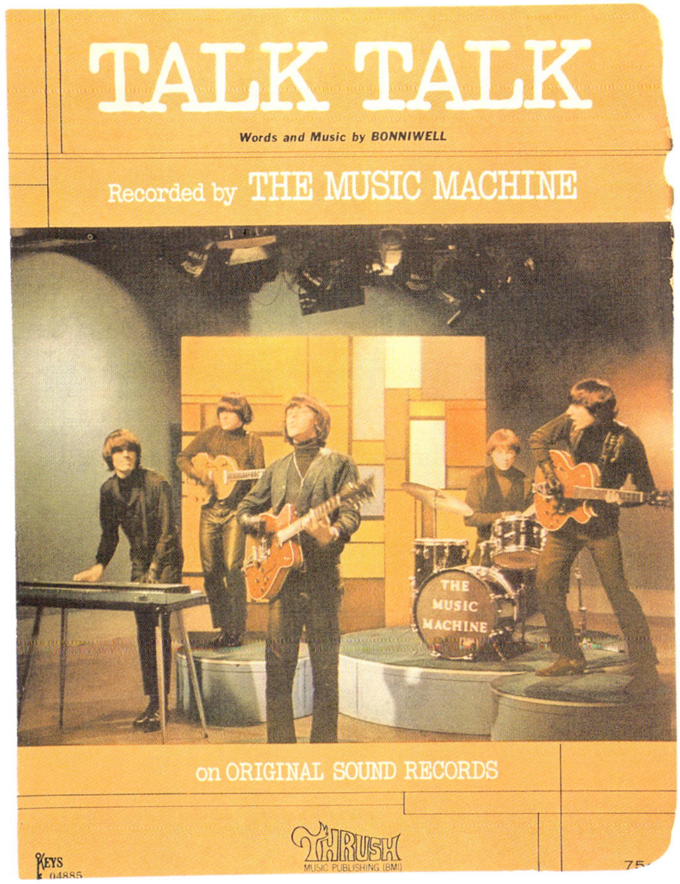


"Talk, Talk" – The Music Machine. Highest charting song for this group from Los Angeles. The sheet pictured here has been quite abused and has little or no value in this condition. Printed in January of 1967. 8.5" x 11", $20-25.

"Pictures of Matchstick Men" – Status Quo. Generally more popular in their native Britain than in the United States, this group did manage to reach number twelve on the American charts with this song in 1968. 9" x 12", $25-35.

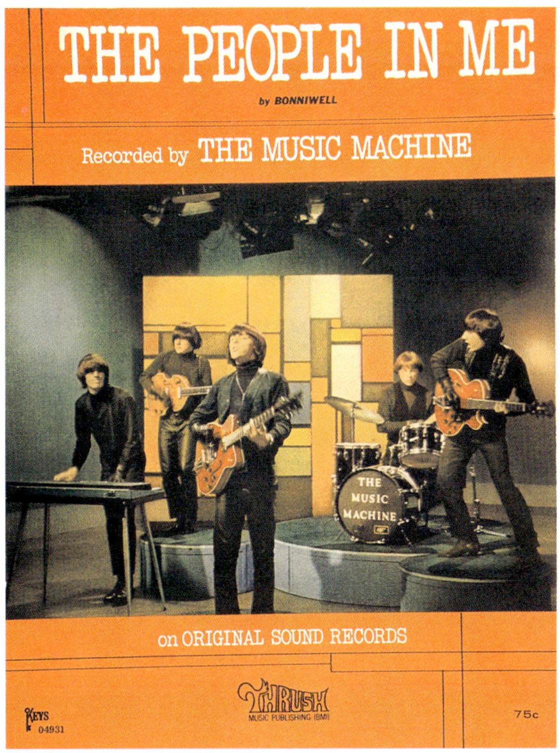


"The People in Me" – The Music Machine. Using the same picture as "Talk, Talk," this sheet shows the band in their usual black clothing. Each band member is also wearing a single black glove. 8.5" x 11", $20-25.

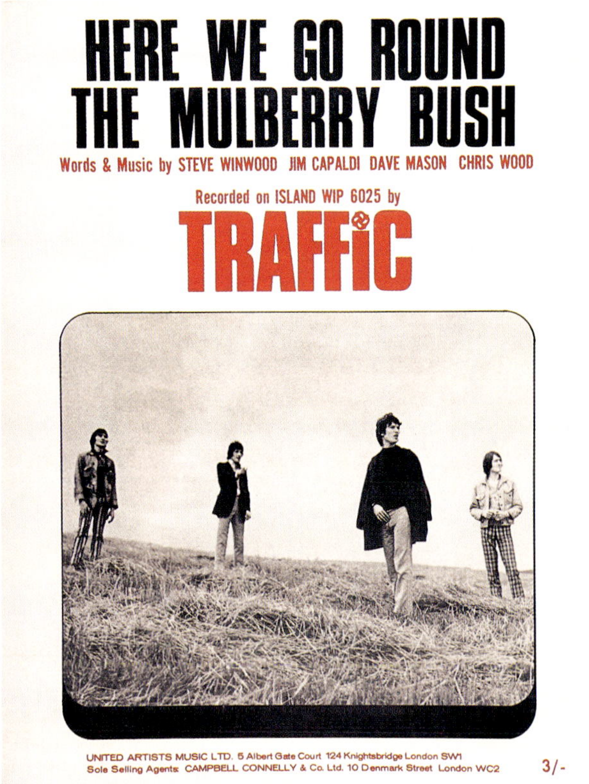


"Here We Go Round the Mulberry Bush" (U.K.) – Traffic. Theme song from the British film of the same name. The band featured multi-talented Steve Winwood just after his departure from the Spencer Davis Group. There is no U.S. counterpart to this sheet music. 8.5" x 11", $15-20.

"I Had Too Much To Dream" – The Electric Prunes. Sizable single that has been categorized as garage, psychedelic, and punk all at the same time. The song started its climb up the charts at the end of 1966 and this sheet was printed in February of 1967. 8.5" x 11", $35-45.

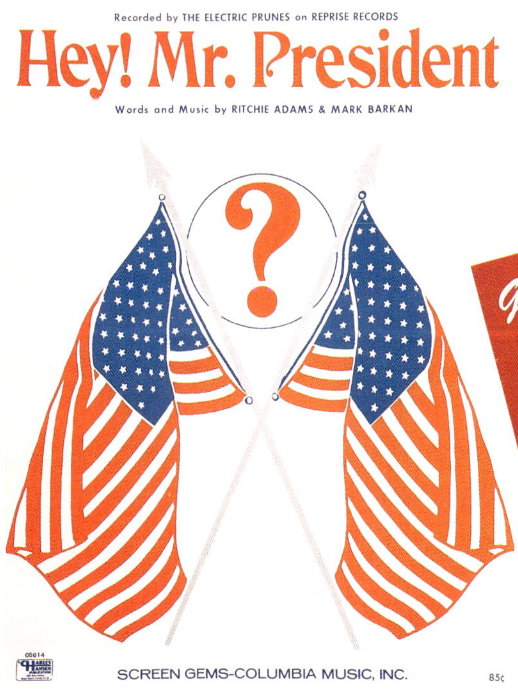


"Hey! Mr. President" – The Electric Prunes. Great American imagery decorates the cover on this still timely tune that questions whether a newly elected president will live up to all of his promises. 8.5" x 11", $15-25.

"Get Me to the World On Time" – The Electric Prunes. This song uses a cover photo taken at the same session as the one used on the sheet music for "I Had Too Much To Dream (Last Night)." Both songs were included on the band's debut album. 9" x 12", $35-45.

"Born To Be Wild" – Steppenwolf. From their debut album; song that is credited with the first use of the term "heavy metal." 9" x 12", $20-30.

"Sit Down, I Think I Love You" – The Mojo Men. This song was written by Stephen Stills for his then band The Buffalo Springfield. This sheet is uncommon and quite desirable. 8.5" x 11", $35-45.

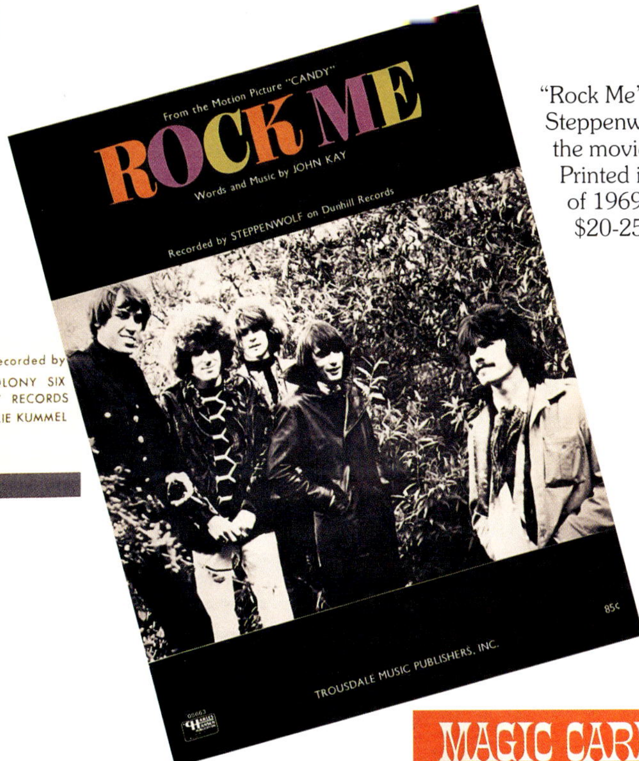


"Rock Me" – Steppenwolf. From the movie *Candy*. Printed in February of 1969. 8.5" x 11", $20-25.

"I Will Always Think About You" – The New Colony Six. Minor late 1960s hit; printed in April of 1968. 8.5" x 11", $20-30.

"Magic Carpet Ride" – Steppenwolf. Number three hard rock hit off the band's second album. 8.5" x 11", $20-35.

Chapter Four

# "Lightnin' Strikes"

## Pop and Rock

Pop and rock are certainly two of the most common categories in popular music and very often interchangeable, depending on which expert or book you consult. There is a great deal of variety in a chapter such as this. Musically, many artists just don't fit specifically into a sub group/style so they end up in the larger, more general category of rock or pop. Originally, pop music was any popular music, but it has, over time, taken on a style of its own. It is generally used to describe light, enjoyable tunes with love, or lack thereof, as a common theme.

Rock music, or rock and roll, is thought to have a slightly harder edge than pop, but it certainly doesn't fall into the category of hard rock. Rock music has its origin in a variety of styles but it is characterized by a high energy level with a beat to match. Value and desirability of the sheet music in these categories will vary greatly.

"Suspicious Minds" – Elvis Presley. Gorgeous photo of "The King" in action. Printed in full color on glossy paper. 8.5" x 11", $30-35.

"These Boots Are Made For Walkin'" (Australia) – Nancy Sinatra. Colorized black and white photo of Ms. Sinatra in those famous boots. The same cover was used on sheet music printed in the U.S., the U.K., and this copy, which is from Australia. 8.5" x 11", $10-15.

"Red Rubber Ball" – The Cyrkle. Co-written by Paul Simon from Simon and Garfunkel. Printed in July of 1966. 8.5" x 11", $20-30.

"Young Girl" – The Union Gap. Cute and descriptive depiction of a drawing that might be done by a young girl. The band photo is small and to the side and is of lesser importance than the drawing itself. 8.5" x 11", $15-20.

"Lady Willpower" – The Union Gap. Number two hit in 1968, written by hit songwriter Jerry Fuller and printed in August of that year. 8.5" x 11", $15-20.

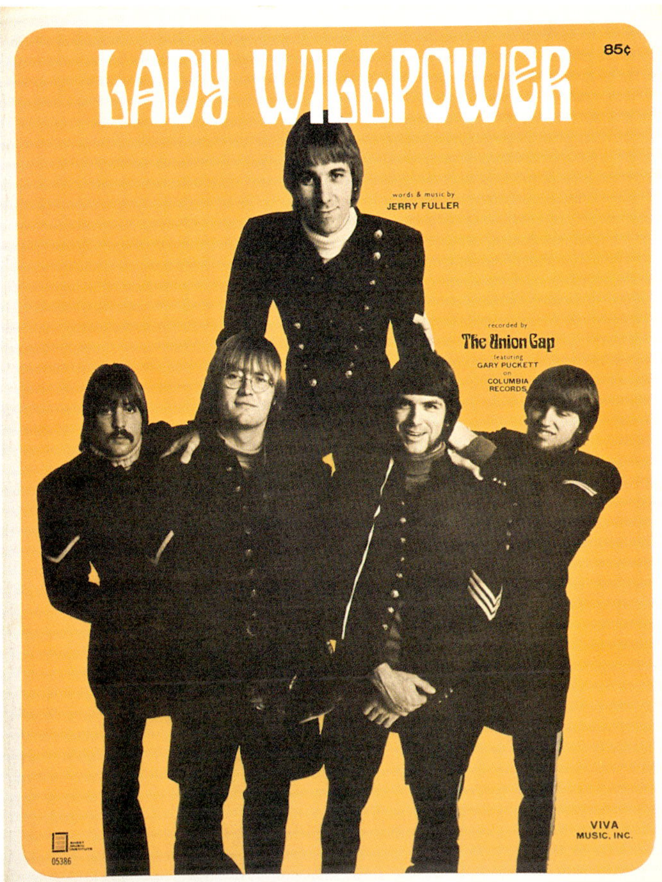

"Over You" – Gary Puckett and The Union Gap. Superb full color photo of the band in their Civil War uniforms. 8.5" x 11", $15-20.

"Woman, Woman" – Gary Puckett and The Union Gap. Common sheet from February of 1968. This song was the first single for the band, traveling as high as number four on the pop charts. 8.5" x 11", $15-20.

"Shakin' All Over" – The Guess Who. Originally known as Chad Allan & the Expressions, the band was renamed after "Guess Who?" was written on the album cover in a vain attempt to fool the record buying public. On the sheet music, the band's name is misspelled as The Guess Who's. 9" x 12", $30-45.

Misspelling of the band's name. It should simply read, The Guess Who.

Recorded by
The GUESS WHO'S
on Sceptor Records

"Sheila" – Tommy Roe. Spirited rocker in the tradition of Buddy Holly. Written by Tommy Roe. 9" x 12", $30-45.

"Palisades Park" – Freddy Cannon. Uncommon printing of this number three hit, showing a photo of Freddy appropriately posed in front of a cannon. Written by Chuck Barris, host of *The Gong Show*. 9" x 12", $25-30.

"Action" – Freddy Cannon. Theme song from the popular 60s TV show *Where the Action Is*. Photo shows Cannon posed in front of something related to his unusual name—cannon balls. 8.5" x 11", $15-20.

"I Got You Babe" (U.K.) – Sonny & Cher. Unusual handwritten title on this sheet music from the United Kingdom shows an intimate photo of the then-married duo. 8.5" x 11", $20-25.

"More Today Than Yesterday" – The Spiral Starecase. The only hit from their only album. The photo is taken directly from the album cover. The band's name is misspelled on the sheet music as The Spiral Staircase. 8.5" x 11", $20-25.

"The Beat Goes On" – Sonny & Cher. The biggest hit from their third album, *In Case You're In Love*. 9" x 12", $15-30.

"Laugh at Me" (U.K.) – Sonny Bono. Half the team of Sonny & Cher, Bono gets the only billing here. The United Kingdom release of "I Got You Babe" uses a similar cover treatment. 8.5" x 11", $10-15.

"Bang Bang (My Baby Shot Me Down)" – Cher. Released as a solo song for Cher in 1966, but written and produced by Sonny Bono. 9" x 12", $15-25.

"But You're Mine" (U.K.) – Sonny & Cher. Went to number fifteen in the United States and number seventeen in Britain. Photo shows the couple in matching shirts and Sonny is wearing his famous fur vest. 8.5" x 11", $10-15.

"Sherry Don't Go" – The Lettermen. Popular adult contemporary group of the time. From the album *Special Request*. 8.5" x 11", $10-15.

"Let's Dance" (New Zealand) – Chris Montez. Rare foreign printing of this 1962 top ten hit. The exact same cover was used on the United Kingdom printing. 8.5" x 11", $10-15.

"Windy" – The Association. Interesting choice for a cover photo as you can hardly see the band for the trees. This song went to number one in 1967. 8.5" x 11", $10-20.

"Along Comes Mary" – The Association. Strange cover layout shows the photo of the songwriter more prominently than the band that made it a hit. 9" x 12", $10-20.

"Cherish" – The Association. "Cherish" went all the way to number one in August of 1966. This sheet was printed in September of that year. 8.5" x 11", $10-20.

"Never My Love" – The Association. Inspired by the real life proposal of one of the songwriters to his girlfriend; went to number two in 1967. 9" x 12", $10-20.

"Sugar Shack" – Jimmy Gilmer & The Fireballs. "Sugar Shack" was the number one single of 1963. The cover shows only Gilmer, with the Fireballs nowhere to be found. 9" x 12", $15-25.

"You've Made Me So Very Happy" – Blood, Sweat & Tears. 1969 number two hit off the second album by this nine man band from New York. 9" x 12", $10-15.

"Candy Girl" (Australia) – The Four Seasons. Single color printing, so common in sheet music from Australia, shows up again on this sheet with a cotton candy pink cover. Note that on foreign printings the band's name is spelled out instead of using the numeral "4". Printed in 1966. 8.5" x 11", $10-15.

"I've Got You Under My Skin" (U.K.) – The Four Seasons. The 4 Seasons' version of a Cole Porter classic. It was a top ten hit for them in 1966. 8.5" x 11", $10-15.

"C'Mon Marianne" – The 4 Seasons. Top ten hit from the LP *New Gold Hits*. 9" x 12", $15-25.

"Big Girls Don't Cry" – The 4 Seasons. Early United States printing of a song that went to number one on both the Pop and R&B charts. 8.5" x 11", $15-35.

"Dawn (Go Away)" – The 4 Seasons. Common sheet music with an even more common photo of the band. This picture showed up on various other titles of their sheet music (in different colors), including "Ronnie" and "Rag Doll." 9" x 12", $15-20.

"Different Drum" – The Stone Poneys. Written by Michael Nesmith of The Monkees. Cover shows a photo of the band along with a drawing of a drum, and yes, even some stones. Printed in January of 1968. 8.5" x 11", $15-30.

Before their disco efforts in the 1970s, The Bee Gees were a five man pop group with a string of top twenty hits during 1967 and 1968. The additional members parted company with the band around 1969, but the brothers continued on, becoming much more successful as a trio than they ever were as a quintet. Their sheet music releases from the 1960s are often more sought after than later ones, with "To Love Somebody" being the most coveted.

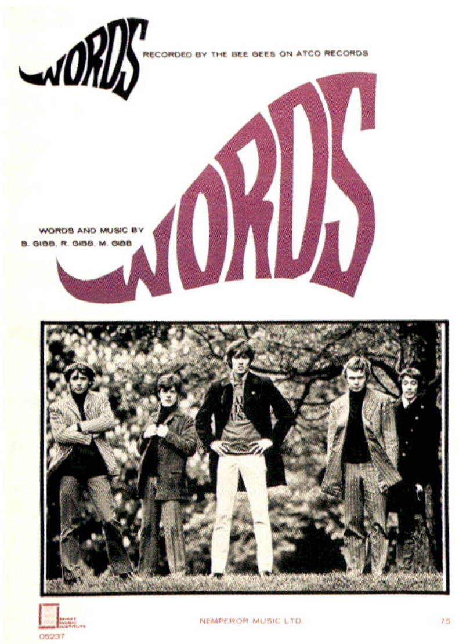


"Words" – The Bee Gees. A unique design was used for the title of this song. It was very much in keeping with the styles that were popular at the time. 8.5" x 11", $20-35.

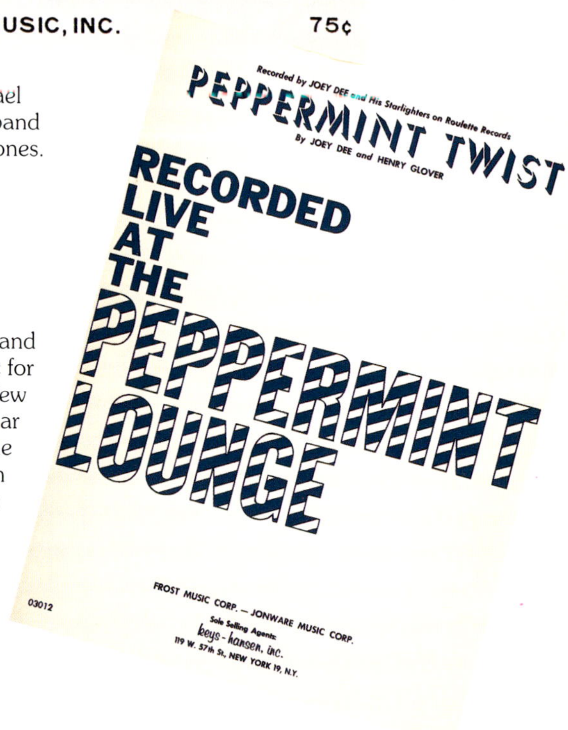


"Peppermint Twist" – Joey Dee and His Starlighters. The sheet music for this song was printed in a few different styles, including a similar cover in red ink (minus the "recorded live") and also in an 8.5" x 11" size featuring a photo of Joey Dee. 9" x 12", $10-15.

"Massachusetts (The Lights Went Out In)" (U.S. and U.K.) – The Bee Gees. Although originally from England, the Bee Gees began by making records in Australia. The U.K. version of this sheet music shows the title in its original form; the U.S. version is reversed. The song went all the way to number one on the British charts. The U.S. sheet was printed in November of 1967. Both 8.5" x 11", U.S. $15-25; U.K. $10-20.

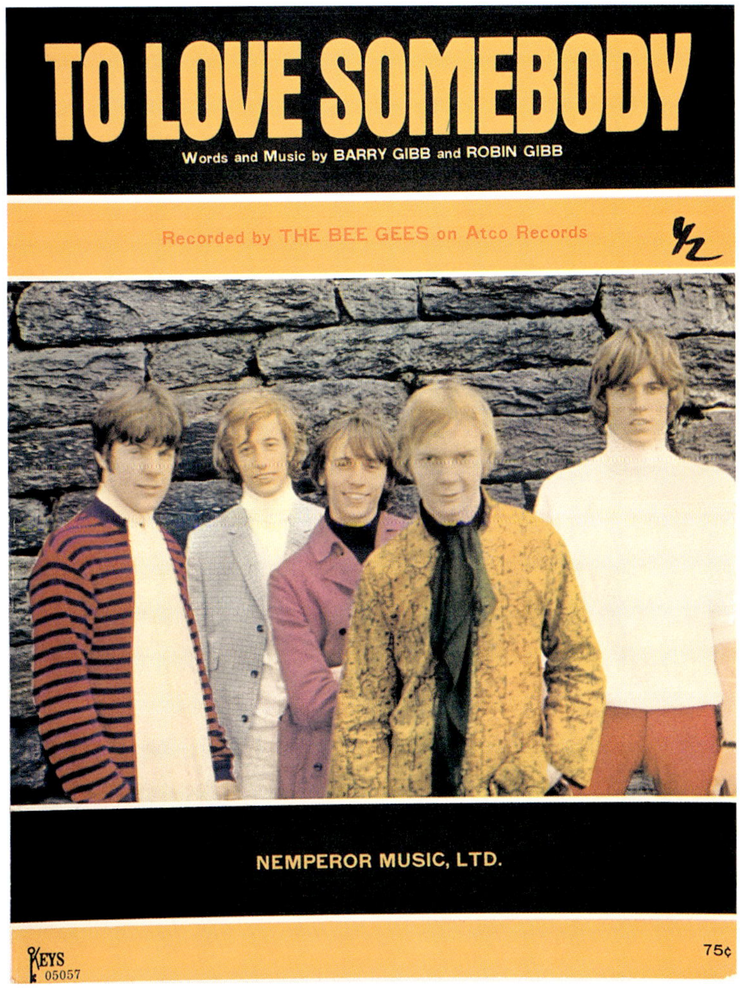


"To Love Somebody" – The Bee Gees. Colorful photo of the band from 1967. This song, although still heard frequently on oldies radio stations in the United States, only went as high as number seventeen on the Billboard® charts the year it was released. 8.5" x 11", $20-40.

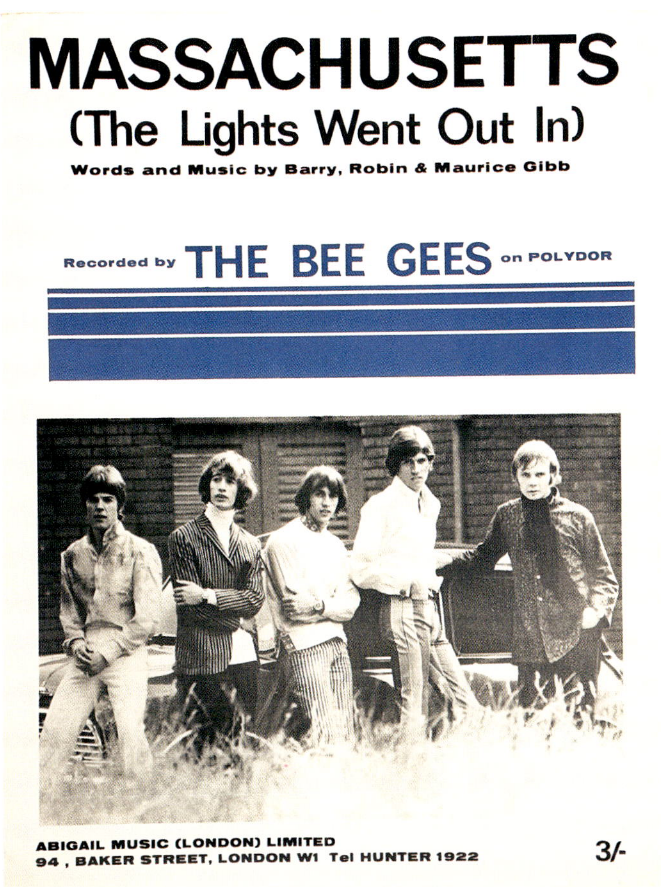

"Holiday" – The Bee Gees. From the album *Bee Gees 1st*. This sheet was printed in October of 1967. 8.5" x 11", $20-30.

"From Now On (Immortal Invisible)" (U.K.) – Flaming Youth. Odd, and somewhat uninteresting, cover for a very unusual song. It merits inclusion here due to the fact that the drummer for this band was none other than Phil Collins of Genesis. *Ark 2* is the title of the LP. 8.5" x 11", $7-12.

"I Fought the Law" – The Bobby Fuller Four. Top ten hit from the album of the same name. Fuller died in 1966 at the age of twenty-two under mysterious circumstances. 9" x 12", $30-50.

"Hey! Baby!" (U.S. and Australia) – Bruce Channel. Number one hit from 1962 that features Delbert McClinton on harmonica. The U.S. sheet was printed in February of that year with an original selling price of 60¢. The Australian sheet was printed without a photo of the artist, but it is still quite appealing due to the delightful drawing of a young girl. Both 8.5" x 11", U.S. $20-35; Australia $15-20.

"Kind of a Drag" – The Buckinghams. From the album of the same name, this was the band's first breakout hit, going all the way to number one in 1967. 9" x 12", $30-40.

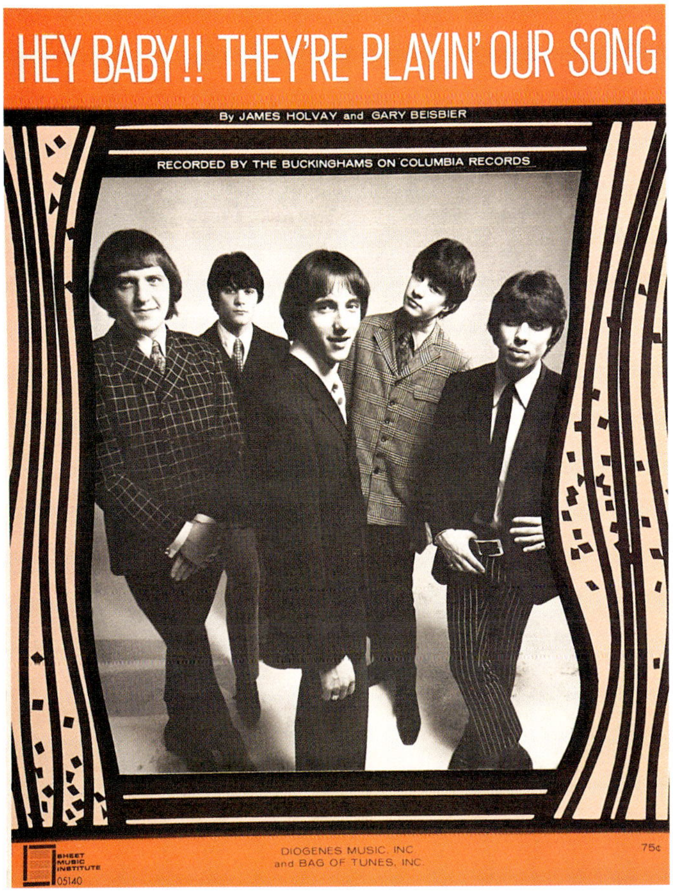


"Hey Baby!! They're Playin' Our Song" – The Buckinghams. This song features cover graphics that were also used on "Don't You Care?" and was from the album *Portraits*. Printed in October of 1967. 8.5" x 11", $30-40.

"Don't You Care" – The Buckinghams. The sheet music for this song had more than one printing, with the other version showing the same photo and layout but in aqua instead of purple. 8.5" x 11", $20-25.

"Back In Love Again" – The Buckinghams. A lower charting hit for the band in June of 1968, it was written by Martin Grebb, keyboardist for the band. 9" x 12", $10-15.

Inside of the "Back In Love Again" sheet music, showing the title that was obviously influenced by late 1960s psychedelia.

"Go Away Little Girl" – The Happenings. Written by the prolific songwriting team of Gerry Goffin and Carole King; this song by The Happenings reached number twelve in 1966. 8.5" x 11", $15-20.

"See You in September" – The Happenings. The Happenings took this song about summer vacation all the way to number three in 1966. This sheet music was printed in August of that year. 8.5" x 11", $15-20.

"Go Away Little Girl" – Steve Lawrence. This is the original 1962 version of the song covered by The Happenings in 1966. This was the only number one hit for Lawrence, who had a long career in music and television. 8.5" x 11", $7-12.

"The 59th Street Bridge Song (Feelin' Groovy)" – Harpers Bizarre. The words and picture on the cover of this very common sheet have been drawn entirely by hand. The song was written by Paul Simon. 9" x 12", $7-12.

"Georgia Pines" – The Candymen. Originally Roy Orbison's back up band, The Candymen reached number eighty-one with this song in 1967. The cover is decorated with pseudo pine trees. 8.5" x 11", $10-15.

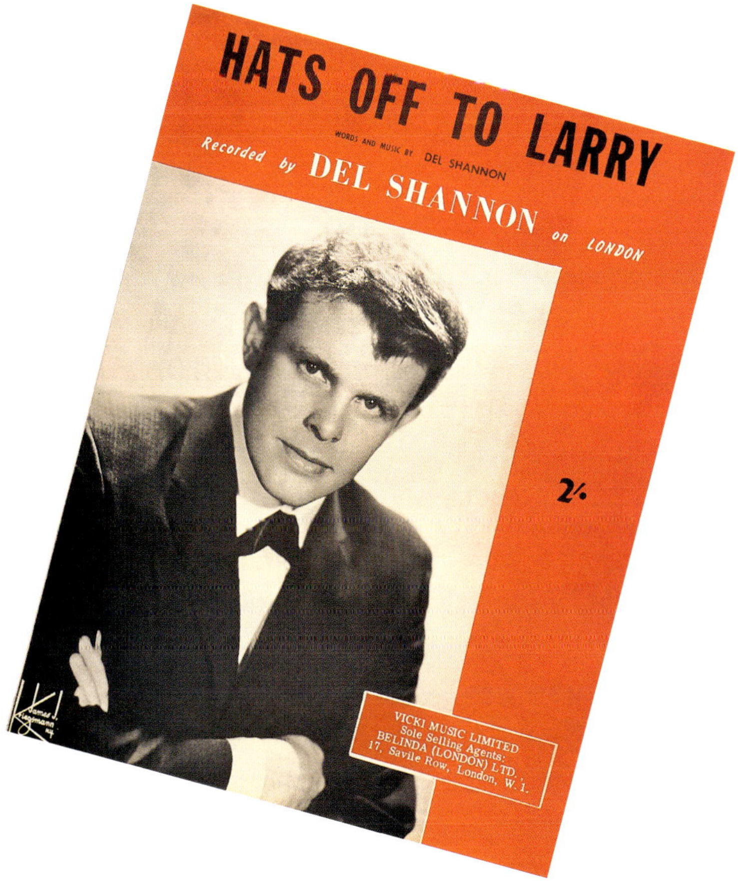


"Hats Off to Larry" (U.K.) – Del Shannon. Second early 1960s hit for Shannon, reaching number five in the United States and number six on the British charts. The same cover was used for the U.K. printing of "Runaway," but with blue instead of red. 8.5" x 11", $10-15.

"Western Union" – The Five Americans. Written by the band themselves, "Western Union" has an unmistakable Morse code chorus. Instead of using a photo of the band, the printers used this old fashioned drawing of a telegram. This odd picture decreases the value of the sheet. 8.5" x 11", $10-15.

"Ways" – The Candymen. A second single from The Candymen that did not reach the Billboard® charts at all. 8.5" x 11", $10-15.

The story of Tommy James and The Shondells started years before their song "Hanky Panky" became a hit in 1966. That song was originally released in 1963, but it wasn't until about three years later that the tune was rediscovered and really took off, launching a career that lasted through the end of the decade. From that serendipitous beginning, song after song became a success for this band, including their foray into pseudo-psychedelia with hits such as "Crimson and Clover" and "Sweet Cherry Wine." Due to their popularity, most of their sheet music releases can be found without too much difficulty.

"No Communication" – The Five Americans. This song from 1968 also features a Morse code type of refrain in attempt to capitalize on the success of their earlier hit, "Western Union." 8.5" x 11", $10-15.

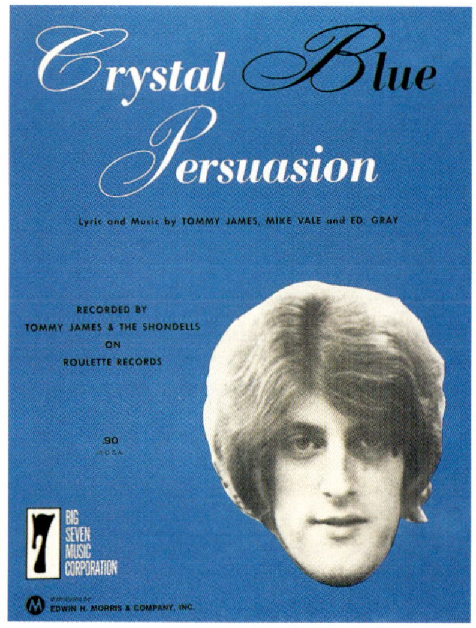


"Crystal Blue Persuasion" – Tommy James and The Shondells. Odd looking cover showing the "floating head" of Tommy James. It climbed to number two in 1969. 8.5" x 11", $7-12.

"Zip Code" – The Five Americans. Another in a line of communication themed songs. The use of zip codes by the postal service was only about four years old at the time of this song's 1967 release. 9" x 12", $10-15.

"Mony, Mony" – Tommy James and The Shondells. The title for this song was taken from the Mutual Of New York insurance building in Manhattan. It went to number three in 1968. 8.5" x 11", $15-25.

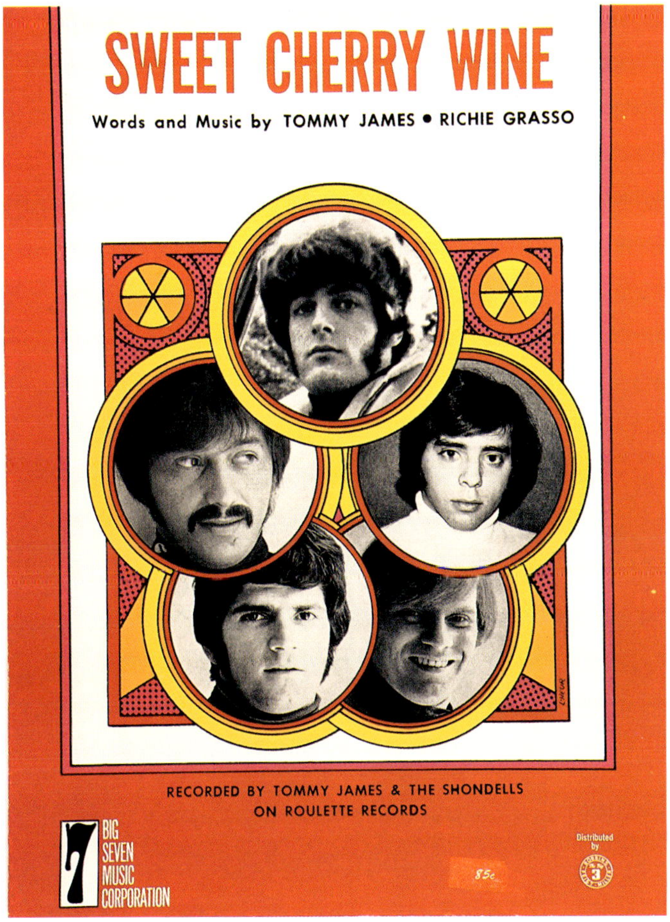


"Sweet Cherry Wine" – Tommy James and The Shondells. From the album *Cellophane Symphony*. 9" x 12", $15-20.

"Mirage" – Tommy James and The Shondells. Curious split photo is used on the cover of this top ten hit from 1967. 8.5" x 11", $10-15.

"Hanky Panky" – Tommy James and The Shondells. Since this 1966 song was such a big hit, the sheet music received more than one printing and can be found in a few color variations, such as yellow (as shown here), purple, and black. 8.5" x 11", $20-25.

"Say I Am (What I Am)" – Tommy James and The Shondells. Cover photo shows the band in matching jackets and pants. Printed in September of 1966. 8.5" x 11", $10-15.

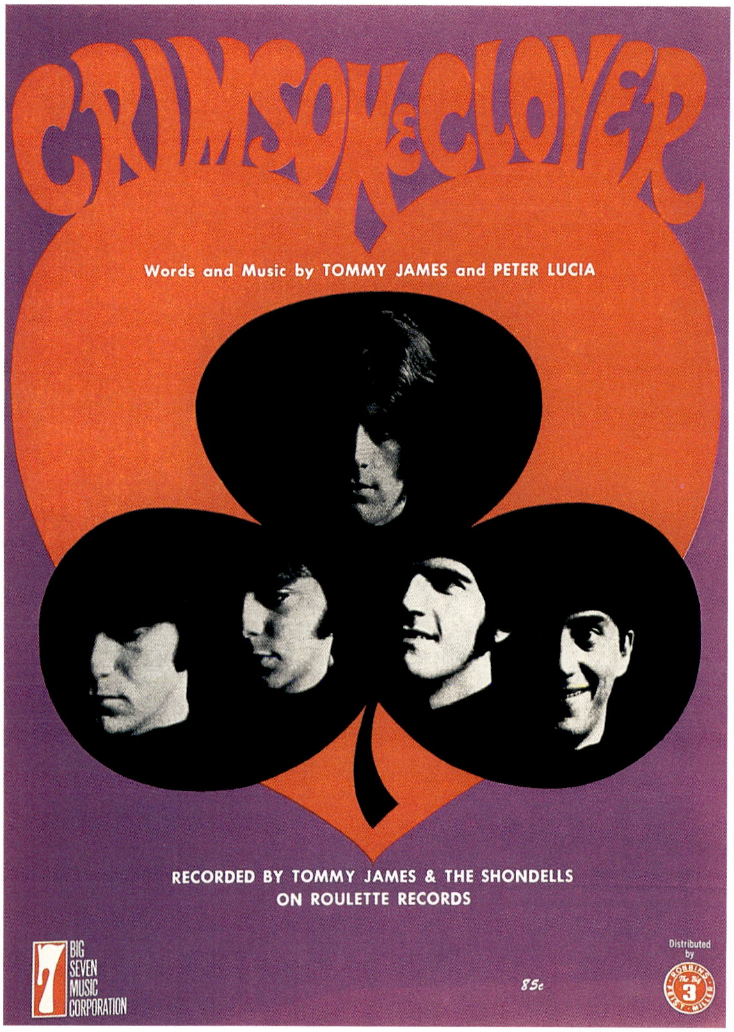


"Crimson & Clover" – Tommy James and The Shondells. "Crimson and Clover" was self produced and had a slightly psychedelic sound. The sheet music uses the heart and clover image from the album cover. 9" x 12", $15-20.

"Arizona" – Mark Lindsay. Top ten solo effort from the lead singer of Paul Revere and The Raiders. The jacket and love beads are the perfect representation of clothing styles from the era. 9" x 12", $15-20.

"I Think We're Alone Now" – Tommy James and The Shondells. Second top ten hit for the group. This sheet was printed in April of 1967. 8.5" x 11", $15-20.

"The Worst That Could Happen" – The Brooklyn Bridge. Number three hit from the band's self titled debut album. Group led by Johnny Maestro, former lead singer of The Crests. 8.5" x 11", $25-45.

"Daydream Believer" – The Monkees. Number one hit for The Monkees in 1967; this sheet music was printed in December of that year. 8.5" x 11", $20-30.

The Monkees were known primarily as a band created for a TV show who didn't play their own instruments; as it turns out, the latter is largely untrue. Beginning with their 1967 album *Headquarters*, the band was playing all their own instruments and writing most of their songs. Over the years, songs that weren't written by the group themselves were written by some of the top pop songwriters of the day, including Boyce & Hart, Goffin & King, and Neil Diamond. Their sheet music ranges from very common to very rare, with prices to match. The two pieces relating to their only movie, *Head*, are the most desirable by far—with prices reaching triple digits.

"A Little Bit Me, A Little Bit You" – The Monkees. The cover for this song written by Neil Diamond shows the group wearing matador costumes in a scene from their popular television show. 8.5" x 11", $15-25.

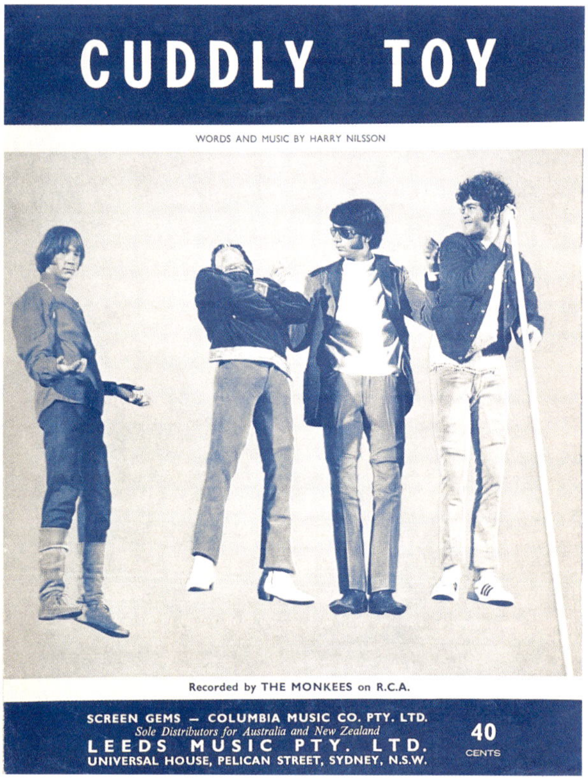


"Cuddly Toy" (Australia) – The Monkees. This is an unusual combination of song and cover photo. The photo is from the group's 1968 movie *Head*. The song "Cuddly Toy" never appeared in the movie or on the soundtrack. 8.5" x 11", $20-25.

"Last Train to Clarksville" – The Monkees. This cover layout was used on various songs from the group's first album including "I'm a Believer," "(Theme From) The Monkees," and "I Wanna Be Free." It is common and not highly prized by collectors. 8.5" x 11", $10-15.

"Valleri" – The Monkees. Unique sheet showing a band photo and various graphics. The picture was taken from their TV show during a performance of a lesser-known tune, "What Am I Doing Hangin' 'Round." 8.5" x 11", $20-40.

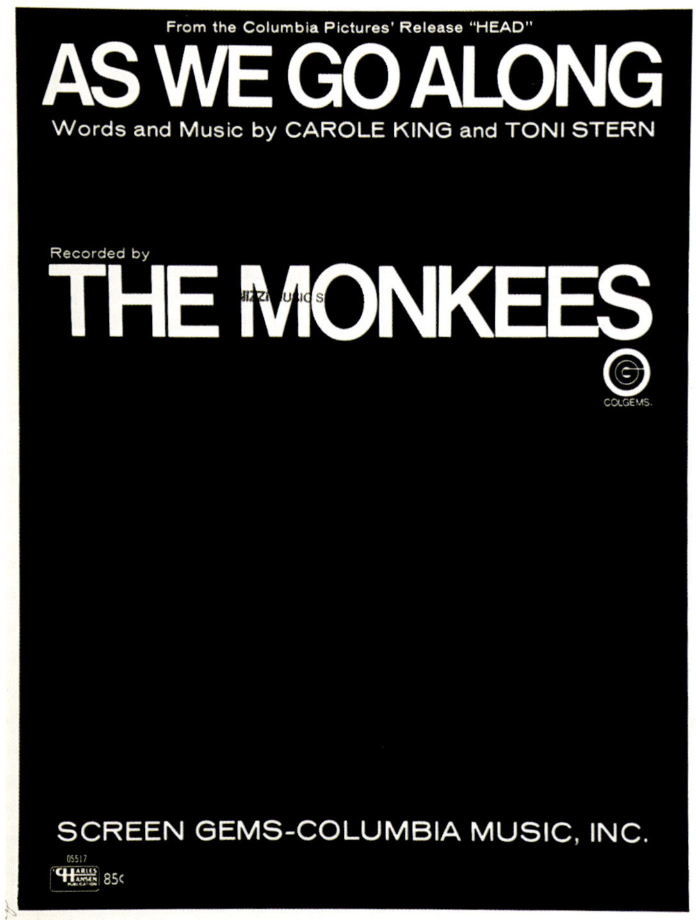


"As We Go Along" – The Monkees. One of the two most valuable pieces of Monkees sheet music; the other being "Porpoise Song." Both pieces are from The Monkees' movie *Head* and have identical cover layouts. 8.5" x 11", extremely rare, $125-150.

"The Girl I Knew Somewhere" – The Monkees. The cover photo for this Michael Nesmith composition shows the group dressed as firefighters. Printed in April of 1967. 8.5" x 11", $20-25.

"Alternate Title" (U.K.) – The Monkees. This is a United Kingdom only printing, since the song was not released as a single in the United States. The original title of this tune, "Randy Scouse Git," was considered too risqué for the British public so an "alternate title" was provided for its overseas release. 8.5" x 11", $20-30.

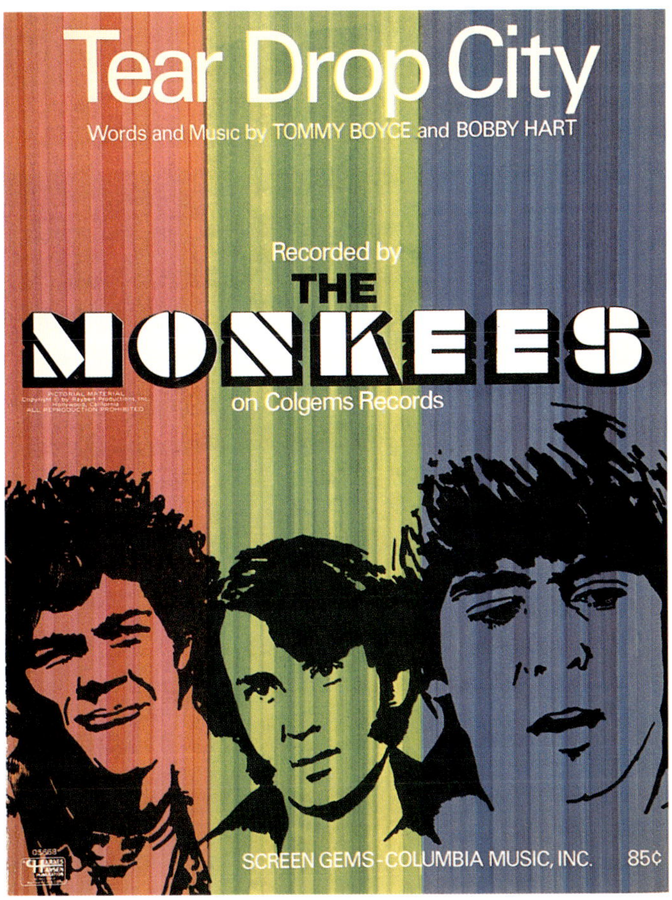

"Randy Scouse Git" (Australia) – The Monkees. Rare sheet music from Australia that uses the original title given to this song. It was also known as "Alternate Title" in the United Kingdom. 8.5" x 11", $10-20.

"Tear Drop City" – The Monkees. Unusual cover design for this late 1960s release. The red, green, and blue lines appear to have been drawn with markers. The U.K. version uses the same cover but was printed in black and white only. 8.5" x 11", $20-35.

"Words" – The Monkees. Written by popular song writing duo Tommy Boyce and Bobby Hart. The same cover was used for the printing of "Pleasant Valley Sunday." 8.5" x 11", $15-20.

"(I'm Not Your) Steppin' Stone" (Belgium) – The Monkees. Very rare sheet music from Belgium. 8.5" x 11", $15-25.

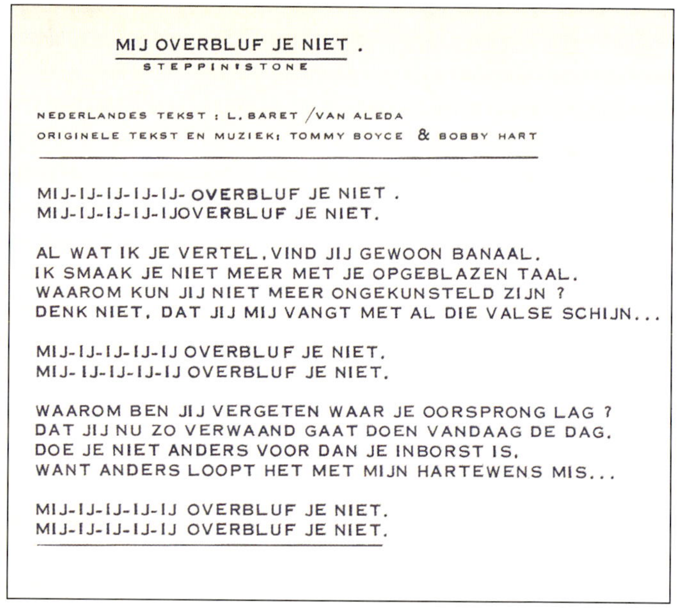

MIJ OVERBLUF JE NIET .

STEPPIN'STONE

NEDERLANDES TEKST : L. BARET /VAN ALEDA
ORIGINELE TEKST EN MUZIEK: TOMMY BOYCE & BOBBY HART

MIJ-IJ-IJ-IJ-IJ- OVERBLUF JE NIET .
MIJ-IJ-IJ-IJ-IJOVERBLUF JE NIET.

AL WAT IK JE VERTEL,VIND JIJ GEWOON BANAAL.
IK SMAAK JE NIET MEER MET JE OPGEBLAZEN TAAL.
WAAROM KUN JIJ NIET MEER ONGEKUNSTELD ZIJN ?
DENK NIET, DAT JIJ MIJ VANGT MET AL DIE VALSE SCHIJN...

MIJ-IJ-IJ-IJ-IJ OVERBLUF JE NIET.
MIJ-IJ-IJ-IJ-IJ OVERBLUF JE NIET.

WAAROM BEN JIJ VERGETEN WAAR JE OORSPRONG LAG ?
DAT JIJ NU ZO VERWAAND GAAT DOEN VANDAAG DE DAG.
DOE JE NIET ANDERS VOOR DAN JE INBORST IS.
WANT ANDERS LOOPT HET MET MIJN HARTEWENS MIS...

MIJ-IJ-IJ-IJ-IJ OVERBLUF JE NIET.
MIJ-IJ-IJ-IJ-IJ OVERBLUF JE NIET.

Back cover of "Steppin' Stone" sheet music from Belgium. The lyrics are written in Dutch.

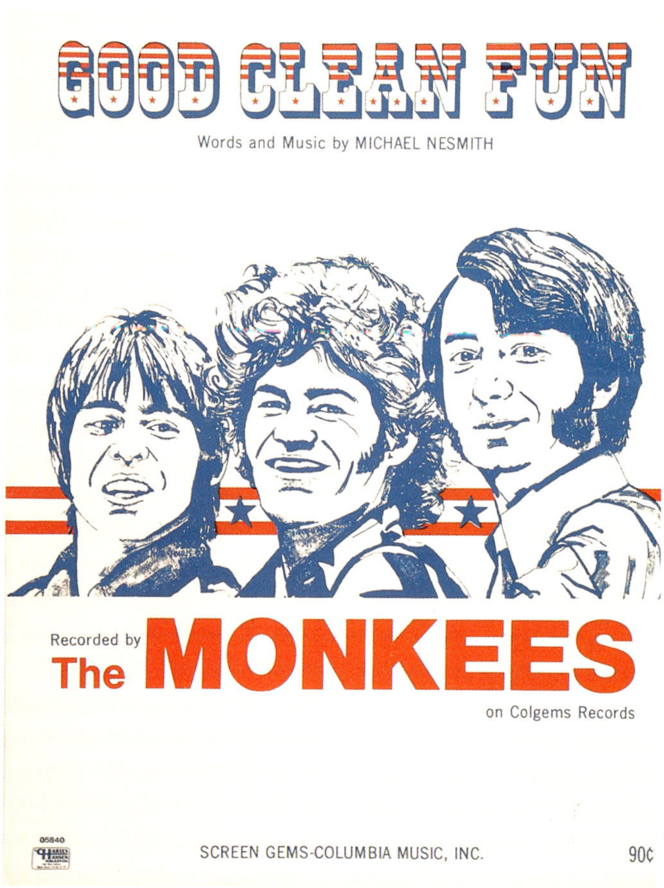


"Good Clean Fun" – The Monkees. The last single released by The Monkees during the 1960s. It shows only three band members, as Peter Tork had left the group by that time. 8.5" x 11", $20-35.

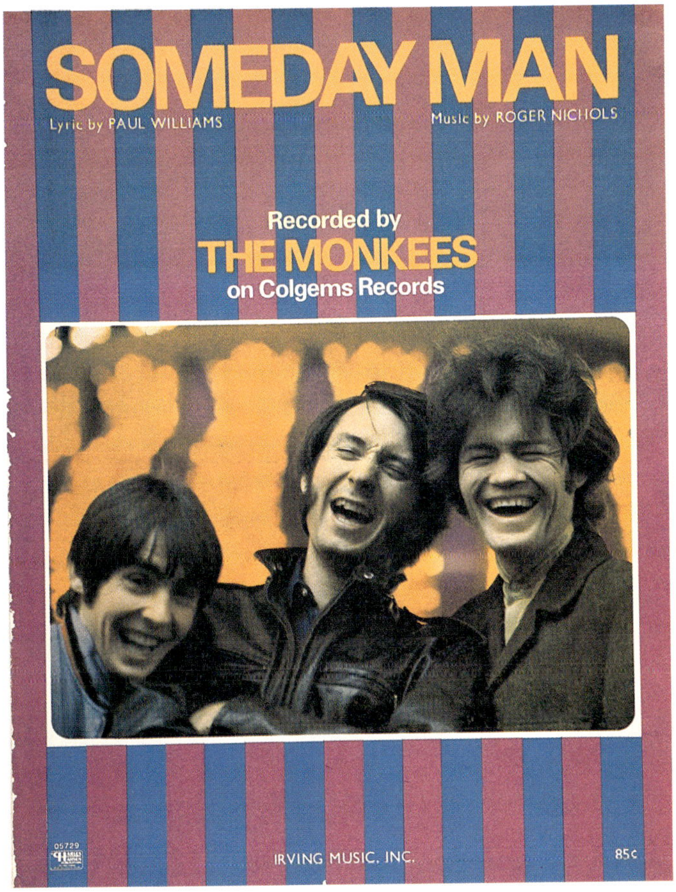


"Someday Man" – The Monkees. The highest chart position this song reached was eighty-one. This sheet music was printed in May of 1969. 8.5" x 11", $20-35.

"(Theme From) The Monkees" – The Monkees. Alternate, and less common, cover for the title song from the group's television show. The other cover is the same as "Last Train To Clarksville." 8.5" x 11", $20-35.

"Finders Keepers" (U.K.) – Cliff Richard and The Shadows. Title song from the 1966 movie that starred both Richard and The Shadows. 8.5" x 11", $10-15.

"I'm a Believer" (U.K.) – The Monkees. The underexposed cover photo comes directly from the pilot episode of *The Monkees* television show. This song, written by Neil Diamond, went to number one in both the United States and Britain. 8.5" x 11", $15-25.

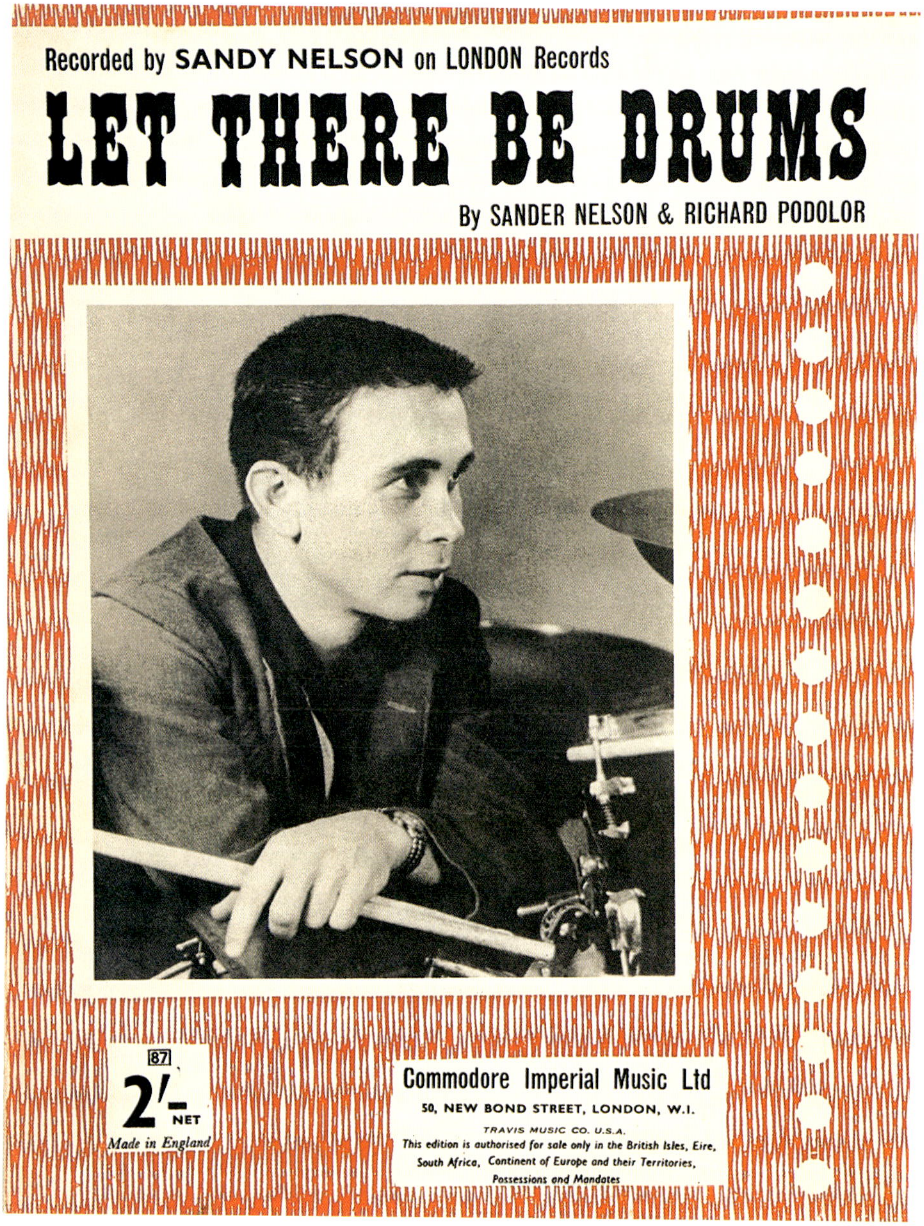


"Let There Be Drums" (U.K.) – Sandy Nelson. This tune gave drummer Nelson an instrumental hit in 1961 in both Britain and the United States. 8.5" x 11", $30-45.

"Shame, Shame" – Magic Lanterns. This British band made the U.S. charts in 1968 with this song about love gone bad. 9" x 12", $10-15.

"In My Book" (Australia) – The Easybeats. This sheet music is unique for two reasons: first, there is no U.S. or U.K. version, and second, the cover photo wraps all the way around the back. Shown here, fully open. 8.5" x 11", $10-20.

"Friday on My Mind" (Australia) – The Easybeats. This is the biggest hit for the band charting as high as number six on the British charts in 1966 and number sixteen on the United States charts in 1967. This sheet uses the exact same photo, front and back. 8.5" x 11", $15-25.

"Love (Can Make You Happy)" – Mercy. The Florida based group recorded this song for a never released movie soundtrack. The ladies from Mercy are pictured on the cover wearing some of the most groovy clothes and hairstyles the late 1960s had to offer. 9" x 12", $10-15.

"She's So Fine" (Australia) – The Easybeats. This 1965 Australia only single was co-written by band member George Young, the older brother of Angus and Malcolm from AC/DC. When opened, as shown here, the cover photo extends around to the back showing all five members of the band. 8.5" x 11", $15-25.

"Somethin' Stupid" – Frank and Nancy Sinatra. Number one hit for this father and daughter team. Printed in August of 1967. 8.5" x 11", $10-20.

"Every Day With You Girl" – The Classics IV. Minor hit for this band from Florida in 1969. 8.5" x 11", $10-15.

"She Drives Me Out Of My Mind" – The Swingin' Medallions. This follow up single to the group's better known hit, "Double Shot of My Baby's Love," was printed in October of 1966. 8.5" x 11", $15-25.

"Stormy" – The Classics IV. Fun photo of the band jammed into a convertible makes this one of the more popular sheets for this group. 8.5" x 11", $15-20.

"Traces" – The Classics IV. This ballad was the biggest hit for The Classics IV. It was printed in February of 1969. 8.5" x 11", $15-20.

"Bad Moon Rising" – Creedence Clearwater Revival. Uncommon sheet with common cover. 8.5" x 11", $10-20.

"Spooky" – The Classics IV. Generic cover does little to enhance the value of this 1968 sheet. 8.5" x 11", $10-15.

"Proud Mary" – Creedence Clearwater Revival. Written by John Fogerty and printed in March of 1969. Ike and Tina Turner had a big hit with this song in 1971. 8.5" x 11", $15-25.

Throughout their career, The Turtles were influenced by a myriad of styles and bands, including The Beatles, surf music, and folk. While the song they are most well known for is "Happy Together," they had a number of other successes as well. Their first single, "It Ain't Me Babe," was written and originally recorded by Bob Dylan. If sheet music exists for The Turtles' recording of this song, it is very rare. Dylan's version of this sheet shows up every now and then and is valued similarly to his other pieces.

"Secret Agent Man" – Johnny Rivers. Written by acclaimed song writing team P.F. Sloan and Steve Barri, this was originally the theme song to a television program. Printed in August of 1966. 8.5" x 11", $15-30.

"Happy Together" – The Turtles. Very common sheet music for this classic song and the band's only number one hit. 9" x 12", $15-25.

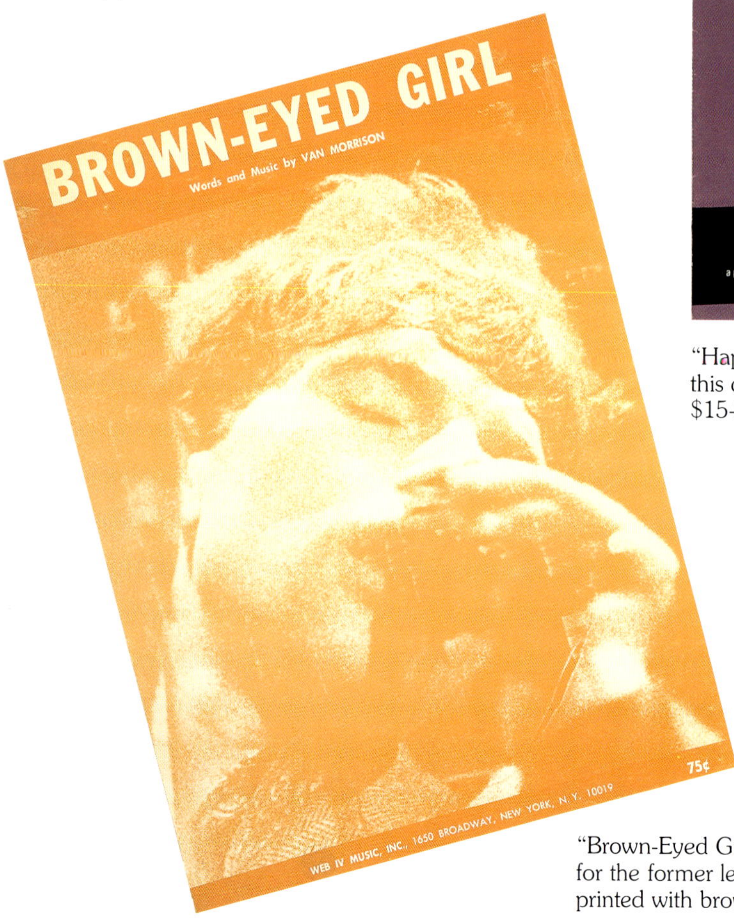


"Brown-Eyed Girl" – Van Morrison. First solo hit for the former lead singer of Them. Appropriately printed with brown ink. 9" x 12", $15-30.

"You Showed Me" – The Turtles. Pop ballad written by two members of The Byrds, Gene Clark and Jim (Roger) McGuinn. 8.5" x 11", $10-15.

"She'd Rather Be With Me" – The Turtles. This follow up to "Happy Together" hit number three on the charts in 1967. 9" x 12", $20-25.

"Elenore" – The Turtles. Cheerful photo of barefoot band members in t-shirts with their names written across the front. 9" x 12", $10-15.

"You Baby (Nobody But You)" – The Turtles. Great black and white cover that conceals the bright, animated nature of this song. 8.5" x 11", $20-25.

"Oh, Pretty Woman" (U.K.) – Roy Orbison. Number one song on both the British and American charts. 8.5" x 11", $10-15.

"Up, Up and Away" – The Fifth Dimension. This "Deluxe Edition" carried a price tag of 99¢ and included music for various instruments. 8.5" x 11", $10-15.

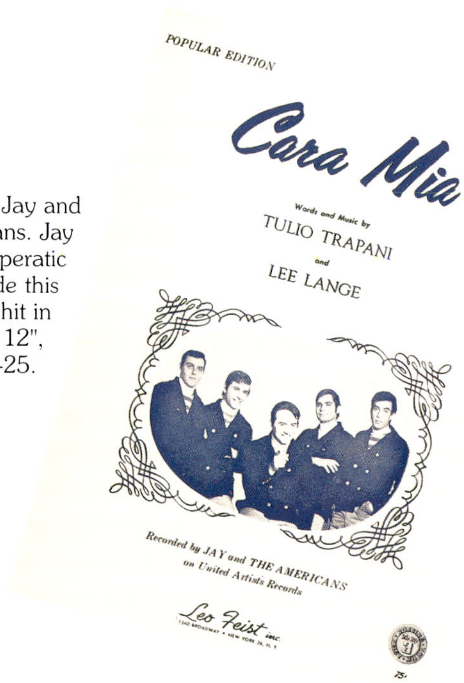


"Cara Mia" – Jay and The Americans. Jay Black's operatic vocal style made this song a big hit in 1965. 9" x 12", $15-25.

"Wedding Bell Blues" – The Fifth Dimension. Band photo features great Sixties wardrobes. Printed in October of 1969. 8.5" x 11", $10-15.

"She Cried" – Jay and The Americans. Recorded with the original "Jay," Jay Traynor, this was the first hit for the band in 1962. 8.5" x 11", $25-40.

"Let's Lock the Door (And Throw Away the Key)" – Jay and The Americans. This sheet had at least one other printing, which showed the same cover layout and photo, only in shades of blue. 9" x 12", $15-20.

"This Diamond Ring" – Gary Lewis and The Playboys. The unusual practice of using "floating heads" to depict the band members was used here with mediocre results. Gary Lewis himself is the only one depicted in full. 9" x 12", $10-20.

"This Magic Moment" – Jay and The Americans. Went to number six in 1969. It was also a hit for The Drifters in 1960. 9" x 12", $15-20.

"Girls In Love" – Gary Lewis and The Playboys. Dynamic and colorful cover makes up for the lack of a photo. 9" x 12", $10-15.

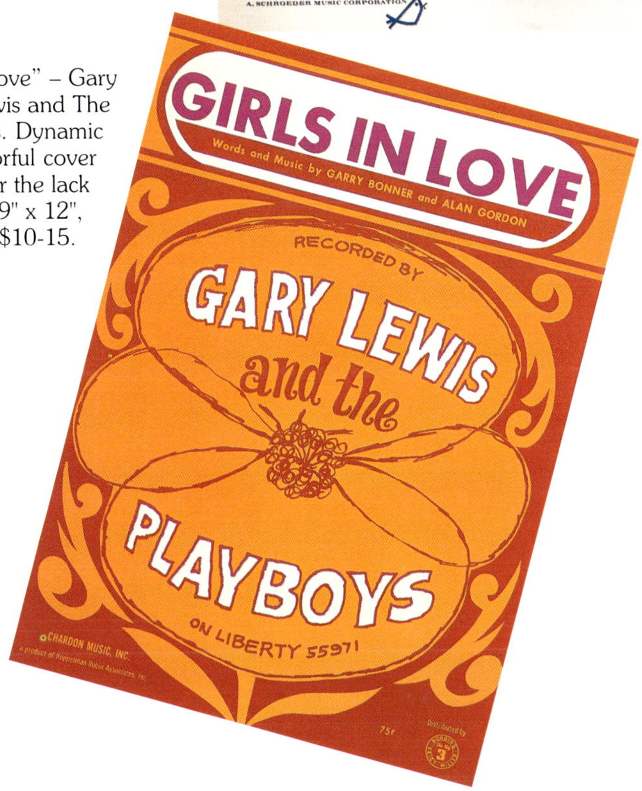

"Save Your Heart For Me" – Gary Lewis and The Playboys. A pleasant photo of Lewis, son of comedian Jerry Lewis, is used on the cover, along with the obligatory hearts. 8.5" x 11", $10-15.

"Come On Down to My Boat" – Every Mothers' Son. Since the song mentions a boat, there is a small drawing of a sailboat, printed in black, at the bottom right hand side of the photo. 8.5" x 11", $15-20.

"Put Your Mind at Ease" – Every Mothers' Son. Funny photo where the band seems to have adopted an additional member. Printed in September of 1967. 8.5" x 11", $10-15.

"Hey! Paula" (U.K.) – Paul and Paula. The duo changed their names from Jill Jackson and Ray Hildebrand (also known as Jill and Ray) to Paul and Paula to coincide with the lyrics. 8.5" x 11", $10-20.

"Daisy Chain" – The Ravens. Descriptive drawing around the title actually shows a chain of daisies. Printed in April of 1964. 8.5" x 11", $10-15.

"Black is Black" (Australia) – Los Bravos. Formed in Spain, this international band reached the top five in the United States with "Black is Black." Considering the popularity of this song, the U.S. sheet music is exceedingly rare, if it exists at all. 8.5" x 11", $15-25.

"Bring a Little Lovin'" – Los Bravos. This sheet music comes up for sale quite often, considering the song itself did not chart well. 9" x 12", $10-15.

"I Don't Care" (Australia) – Los Bravos. Sheet music from Australia printed again in only one color ink, which was very common in that country at that time. 8.5" x 11", $10-15.

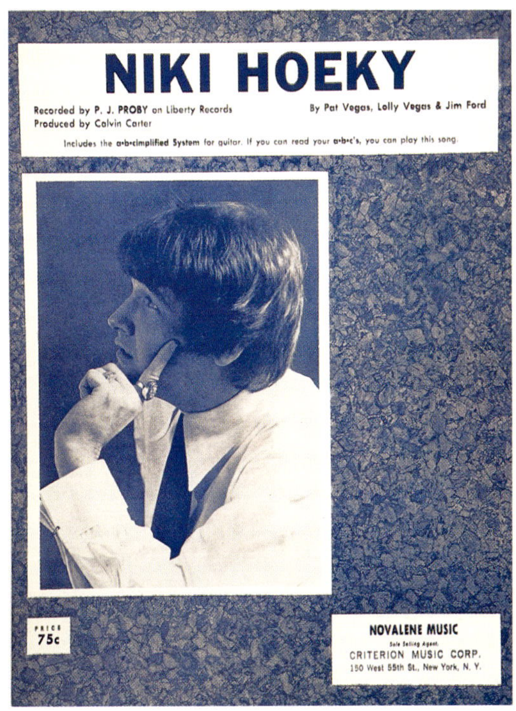


"Niki Hoeky" – P.J. Proby. Standard and somewhat uninteresting cover layout used for this flashy Texas native. This was his only single to do well in the United States. Other songs only fared well in England. 9" x 12", $20-25.

"Pretty Ballerina" – The Left Banke. The exact same cover layout is used on this lesser known recording as was used on their hit, "Walk Away Renee." 8.5" x 11", $15-20.

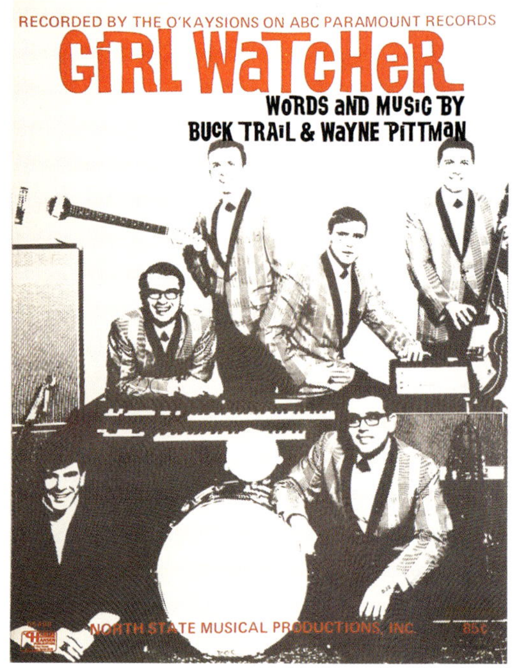


"Girl Watcher" – The O'Kaysions. Top five hit in 1968. Shows the band in matching jackets reminiscent of the early 1960s. 8.5" x 11", $20-25.

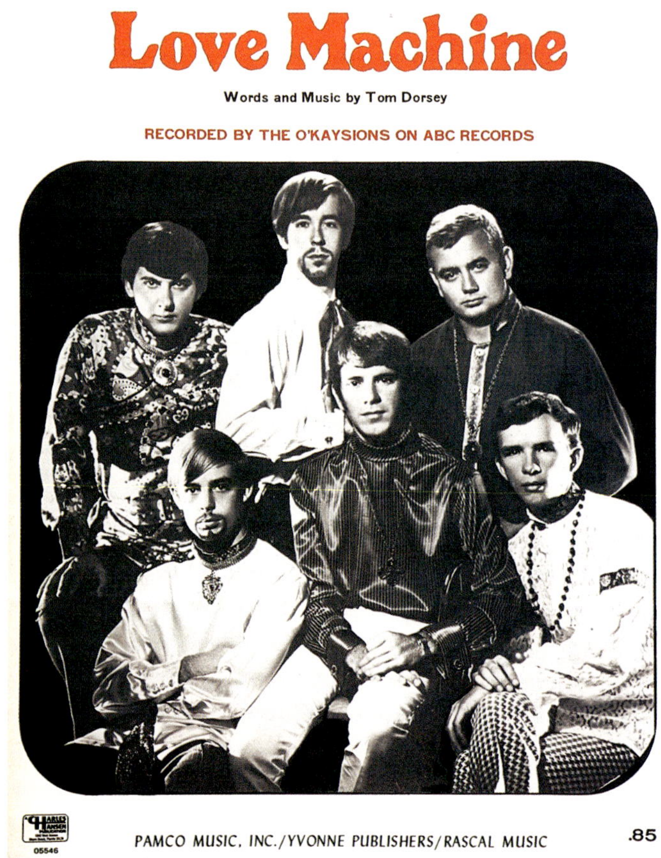


"Love Machine" – The O'Kaysions. Lesser-known song with a photo that shows the band in psychedelic clothing in keeping with the year of the song's release, 1968. 8.5" x 11", $10-20.

"Walk Away Renee" – The Left Banke. Standard cover is used on this hit for the New York based Left Banke. Printed in November of 1966. 8.5" x 11", $20-30.

"My Special Angel" – The Vogues. Cover version of Bobby Helms' 1957 hit. Printed in October of 1968. 8.5" x 11", $10-15.

"Woman Helping Man" – The Vogues. This ballad uses a serious looking photo for this vocal group from Pennsylvania. 8.5" x 11", $10-15.

"The Rain, The Park & Other Things" – The Cowsills. One of two covers for this song; the other shows just the boys in a black and white photo. 9" x 12", $15-25.

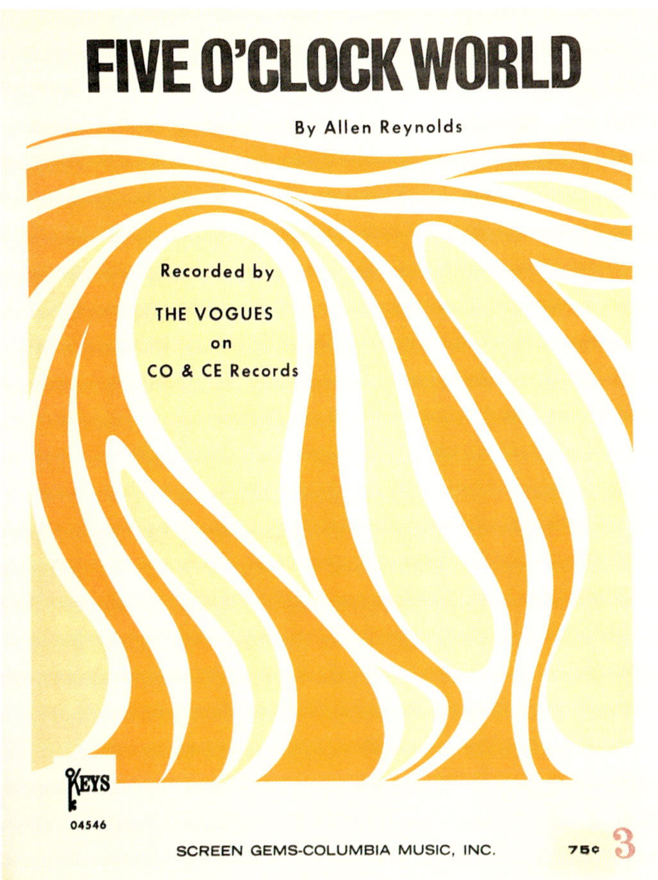

"Indian Lake" – The Cowsills. Fun shot of this family group—mom and her five kids—at an amusement park. The Cowsills were the inspiration for *The Partridge Family* television show. 9" x 12", $10-20

"Five O'Clock World" – The Vogues. Considering the popularity of this song, the sheet music would have benefited from the use of a picture of the band. Different color printings of this style sheet have emerged, but none with a band photo. 8.5" x 11", $10-15.

Chapter Five

# "Going To a Go-Go"

## R&B, Soul, and Motown

While all similar in style, R&B, soul, and Motown each have unique aspects. R&B, or rhythm and blues, evolved in part from blues, jazz, and what is known as jump music. It is generally considered the predecessor to what became rock and roll. Soul music began as a combination of R&B and gospel but has come to encompass a wide variety of similar sounds and styles. Different musicians took soul music in different directions and it began to appeal to a wider audience beyond the traditional African-American fan base. Music produced by white musicians, which is stylistically similar to black soul music, is sometimes called blue-eyed soul.[2] Motown started as an independent label created by Berry Gordy, Jr., but over the years the uniform house sound created by this label became so instantly identifiable that "Motown" unequivocally became a style unto itself.[3]

The sheet music from all of these styles can be desirable to the point where it significantly affects price. Soul, R&B, and Motown each have devoted fans that can be quite dedicated in the pursuit of the music they love. Some of the earlier pieces are very rare and can be rather valuable.

"Hit the Road Jack" (U.K.) – Ray Charles. Lighthearted call and answer song that topped the U.S. charts in 1961. 8.5" x 11", $10-15.

"Hey, Girl" – Freddie Scott. Biggest hit for Scott was released in 1961, with the sheet music being printed in August of that year. 8.5" x 11", $30-40.

"Shotgun" – Jr. Walker and The All Stars. Walker, a saxophone player, had his first big hit with this R&B styled song in 1965. 8.5" x 11", $30-45.

"Someday We'll Be Together" – The Supremes. Diana Ross was the only Supreme to sing on this 1969 record. 9" x 12", $25-30.

While eventually becoming the First Ladies of Motown, The Supremes originally did not have any successful singles until they teamed up with writers/producers Brian Holland, Lamont Dozier, and Eddie Holland in 1964. From there, single after single not only hit the charts but topped them as well, with no less than twelve number ones.

"My World Is Empty Without You" – The Supremes. Always the picture of elegance, The Supremes decorate the 1966 cover of this song written by the stellar writing and producing team of Holland, Dozier and Holland. 9" x 12", $40-60.

"Love Is Here and Now You're Gone" – The Supremes. Pretty pink cover on this 1967 sheet music that sparkles like the ladies themselves. 9" x 12", $25-35.

"Love Child" (U.K.) – The Supremes. Gorgeous photo of the statuesque songbirds in their beaded best. Sheet music is from 1968. 8.5" x 11", $10-15.

"Love Child" (Australia) – The Supremes. Photo on this Australian release shows the group sightseeing, camera in hand. 8.5" x 11", $15-20.

"Love Child" – The Supremes. This photo shows the group dressed in costumes designed to look poor, with matching sweatshirts and torn jeans. 9" x 12", $25-30.

"You Can't Hurry Love" – The Supremes. Great shot showing the singers in true 1960s hair and makeup. This photo was used on more than one of the sheet music releases for the Supremes. 9" x 12", $20-40.

"Stop! In the Name of Love" – The Supremes. Very desirable sheet music for a song that spent two weeks in the number one spot. The photo is cut (almost) into the shape of a heart. 8.5" x 11", $40-60.

"You Keep Me Hangin' On" – The Supremes. The sheet music for this 1966 number one song uses the same photo as was used on "You Can't Hurry Love." 9" x 12", $35-50.

"(Your Love Keeps Lifting Me) Higher and Higher" (U.K.) – Jackie Wilson. 1967 hit for Wilson in the United States. The song charted two years later in Britain. 8.5" x 11", $10-20.

"Raindrops" (U.K.) – Dee Clark. Very unusual sheet music cover for a U.K. printing. This style would normally be found only on a sheet from the United States. The lack of a photograph, however, significantly lowers the value. 8.5" x 11", $7-12.

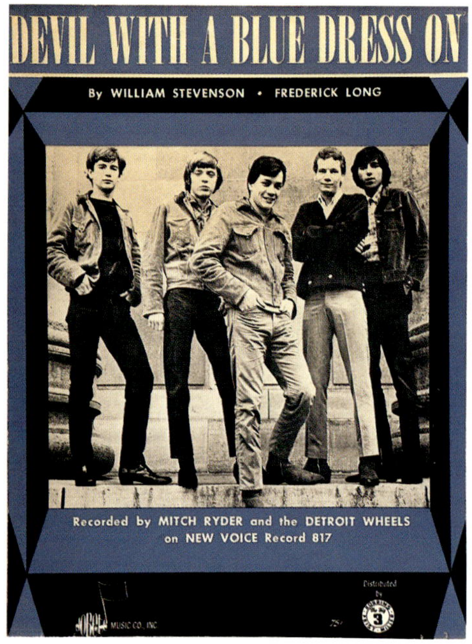


"Devil With a Blue Dress On" – Mitch Ryder and The Detroit Wheels. This song was actually a blend of "Devil With a Blue Dress On" and "Good Golly Miss Molly," although the latter is not mentioned in the title of this 1966 hit. 9" x 12", $20-30.

"The Birds and the Bees" – Jewel Akens. This one hit wonder climbed to number three on the pop charts and to number twenty-one on the R&B charts in 1965. 9" x 12", $15-20.

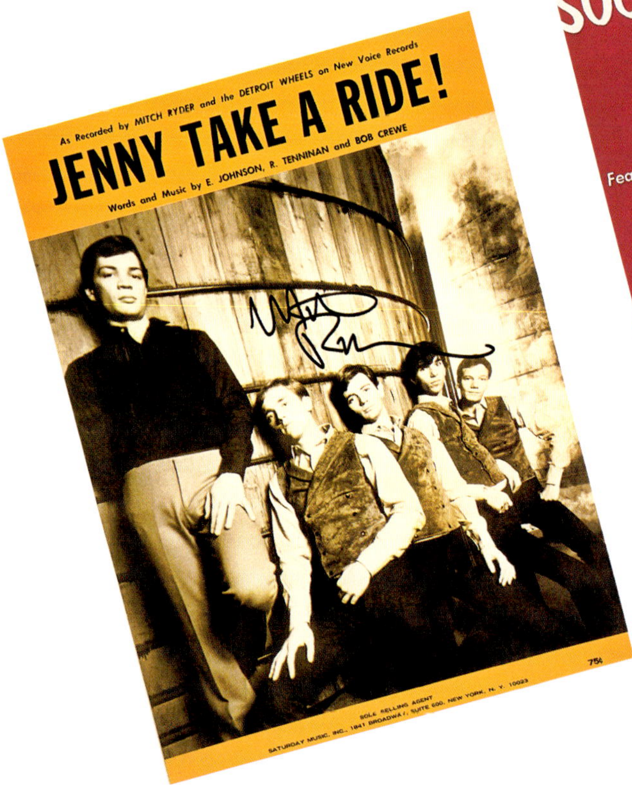


"Jenny Take a Ride!" – Mitch Ryder and The Detroit Wheels. Combination song of "C.C. Rider" by Chuck Willis and "Jenny, Jenny" by Little Richard. This particular sheet was hand signed for the author by Mitch Ryder at the World Trade Center in New York City on August 28, 2001. 9" x 12", value without autograph $25-35.

"Sock It to Me – Baby" – Mitch Ryder and The Detroit Wheels. Mitch Ryder, born William Levise, Jr., is the only one credited on this 1967 sheet music, even though the song was recorded while he was still with The Detroit Wheels. 9" x 12", $20-30.

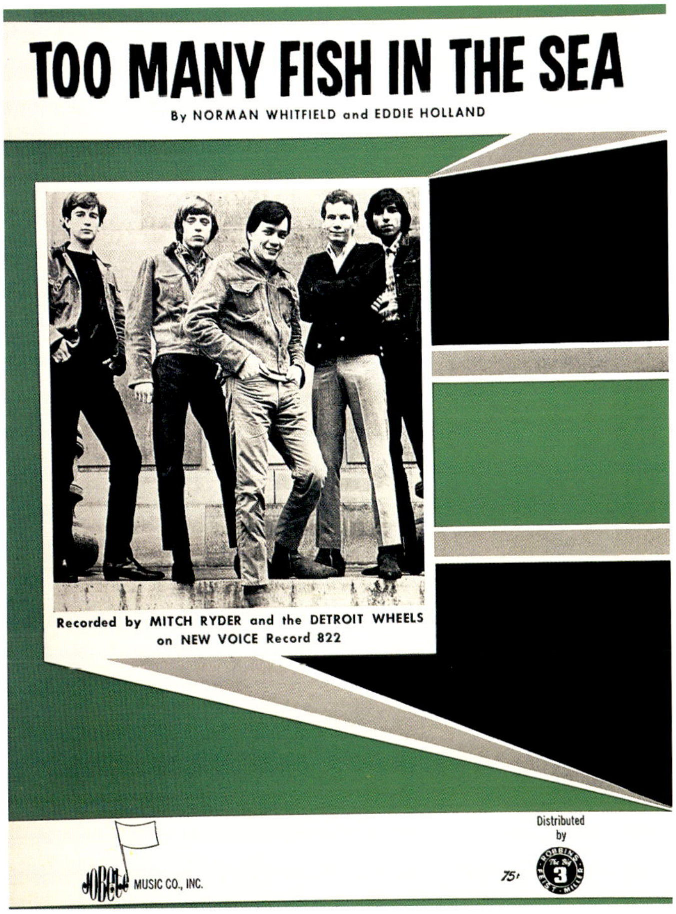


"Too Many Fish in the Sea" – Mitch Ryder and The Detroit Wheels. Same cover photo is used on this 1967 sheet music as was used for "Devil With a Blue Dress On." 9" x 12", $20-30.

"Over, Under, Sideways, Down" (U.K.) – The Yardbirds. Co-written by guitar legend Jeff Beck, who was part of the band for about a year and a half. His name is spelled as "Geoff" in the credits on this 1966 sheet. 8.5" x 11", $20-25.

"(Sittin' On) the Dock of the Bay" – Otis Redding. This 1968 song was a huge hit for Redding, but was, unfortunately, released posthumously. This sheet was printed in April that year. 8.5" x 11", $20-30.

"Little Latin Lupe Lu" – Mitch Ryder and The Detroit Wheels. This song was written by Bill Medley of The Righteous Brothers. Ryder and The Wheels charted with it three years later in 1966. 9" x 12", $20-30.

"For Your Love" (Australia) – The Yardbirds. Keith Relf, lead singer of The Yardbirds, is featured prominently in this photograph. Relf died in 1976 after being electrocuted while playing guitar. The same cover was used on the U.K. printing, with the title and bottom strip in red. 8.5" x 11", $25-30.

"Stay" (U.K.) – Maurice Williams & The Zodiacs. At just about one minute and thirty seconds, this song is the shortest to ever reach number one in the United States. 8.5" x 11", $15-20.

"Slow Twistin'" (U.K.) – Chubby Checker. One of a number of twist-related songs by Checker. This song is from 1962. 8.5" x 11", $7-12.

"For Your Love" – The Yardbirds. First and highest charting single for the band in the United States. The cover layout used for this song is common and is used frequently for other bands and songs. 9" x 12", $25-35.

"Take a Letter Maria" – R.B. Greaves. Greaves, nephew of Sam Cooke, reached number two with this song in 1969. 8.5" x 11", $10-20.

"I Only Want To Be With You" – Dusty Springfield. This debut, breakout release from Ms. Springfield in 1963 has an original selling price of only 60¢. 9" x 12", $25-40.

"Baby, Now That I've Found You" (U.K.) – The Foundations. First release from this multiracial British band. 8.5" x 11", $15-20.

"Build Me Up Buttercup" – The Foundations. This song, featured the 1998 movie *There's Something About Mary*, was originally leased in 1969. 9" x 12", $15-20.

"You Don't Have To Say You Love Me" – Dusty Springfield. The British soul singer charted in both the U.S. and Britain with this Italian song originally titled "Io Che Non Vivo (Senza Te)." 9" x 12", $20-30.

"Sunny" – Bobby Hebb. One of two covers for this sheet music. The other more common cover features a young blonde girl with flowers in her hair. This version was printed in September of 1966. 8.5" x 11", $10-20.

"Judy in Disguise" (U.K.) – John Fred and His Playboy Band. Playful take on The Beatles' "Lucy in the Sky With Diamonds." 8.5" x 11", $15-20.

"Whipped Cream" – The Stokes. Yummy looking cover for this R&B instrumental written by Naomi Neville, a pseudonym for Allen Toussaint. 8.5" x 11", $7-12.

"Cool Jerk" – The Capitols. R&B trio from Detroit took this song to number seven in 1966. 9" x 12", $25-45.

"A Beautiful Morning" – The Rascals. Wonderfully colorful sheet from 1968 showing the band in concert as well as a superimposed studio shot. 9" x 12", $20-35.

The Young Rascals started on the East Coast playing in a number of local R&B bands, eventually uniting into one of America's top Blue Eyed Soul groups. They dropped the "Young" from their name in 1968. Sheet music for any of this group's songs is a real treat! Cover graphics, photos, and colors are all very different from one piece to the next—no two pieces are alike. There are very few other bands that can make that claim, especially with a musical catalog as extensive as theirs.

"How Can I Be Sure" – The Young Rascals. Some of the more outrageous 1960s fashions can be found on the cover of this hit from 1967. 9" x 12", $20-35.

"Groovin'" – The Young Rascals. This song spent four weeks at number one in 1967. 9" x 12", $15-30.

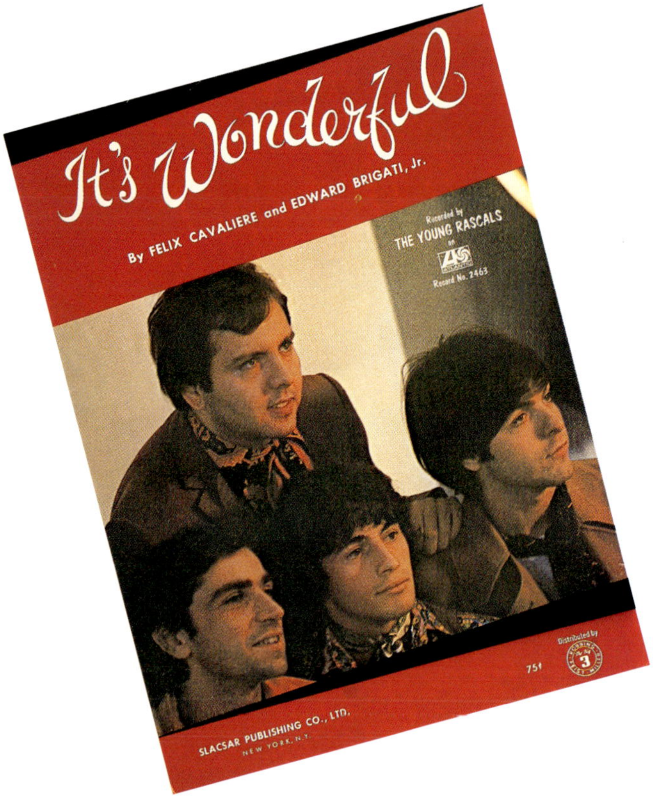


"It's Wonderful" – The Young Rascals. Photo from the same session that produced the cover for "How Can I Be Sure." 9" x 12", $15-25.

"Good Lovin'" – The Young Rascals. Huge hit for The Rascals in 1965. This sheet had more than one printing, with another version having aqua colored stripes. Shows the band name as "The Rascals" but at this early date, they were still called "The Young Rascals." 8.5" x 11", $20-40.

"A Girl Like You" – The Young Rascals. Fun cartoon drawing of the band. 9" x 12", $15-25.

"I've Been Lonely Too Long" – The Young Rascals. Solid color sheet showing the band having fun with dessert. 9" x 12", $15-25.

"See" – The Rascals. Late 1960s release. The lyrics are bursting with hippie imagery of love and nature. 9" x 12", $15-25.

"People Got To Be Free" – The Rascals. Late 1960s anthem of freedom and brotherly love. 9" x 12", $15-25.

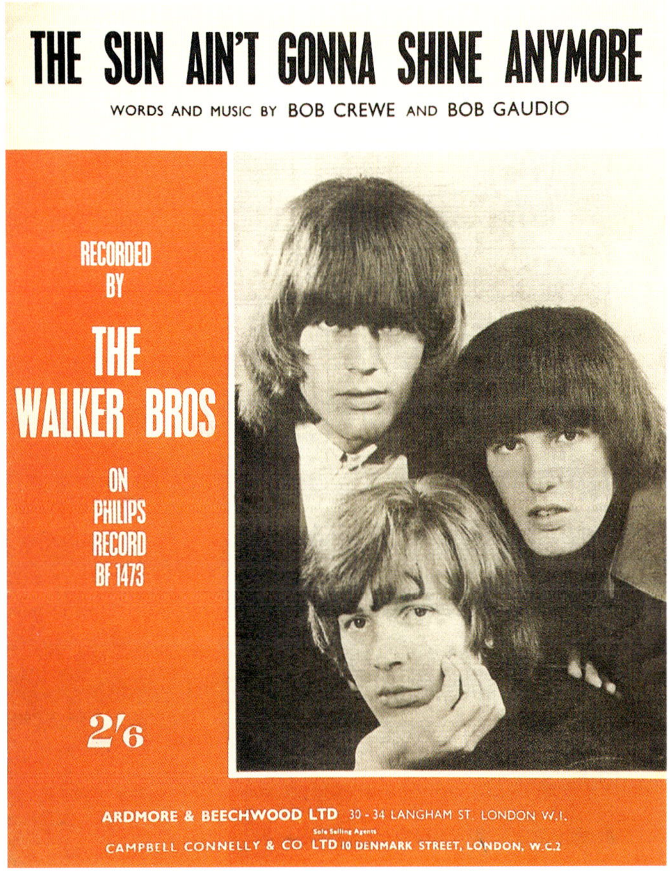


"The Sun Ain't Gonna Shine Anymore" (U.K.) – The Walker Brothers. This American group from California was much more popular in the U.K. than they were in their own country. 8.5" x 11", $20-25.

"Take Good Care Of Her" – Mel Carter. Last and lowest charting hit for Carter. He is most well known for the song "Hold Me, Thrill Me, Kiss Me." 8.5" x 11", $10-15.

"Make It Easy On Yourself" (U.K.) – The Walker Brothers. The Walker Brothers weren't named Walker and weren't brothers. This song was written by the team of Hal David and Burt Bacharach. 8.5" x 11", $20-25.

"Papa's Got a Brand New Bag" (U.K.) – James Brown. Early photo of "The Godfather of Soul" playing the drums. 8.5" x 11", $10-20.

"Expressway To Your Heart" – Soul Survivors. Top five hit for the band in 1967. 9" x 12", $15-25.

"The Name Game" (Australia) – Shirley Ellis. Co-written by Ellis, this song had people all over the world adding their name to the game. 8.5" x 11", $10-15.

"Everlasting Love" (Australia) – The Love Affair. This five member band from London took this tune all the way to number one on the British charts in 1968. 8.5" x 11", $10-15.

"Rainbow Valley" (U.K.) – The Love Affair. Second hit for the band in 1968. This sheet music is unusual for the U.K. with its use of bright rainbow colors. 8.5" x 11", $10-15.

"Baby, Baby, Don't Cry" – Smokey Robinson & The Miracles. In 1967, the group changed their name from "The Miracles" to "Smokey Robinson & The Miracles." This song is from 1969. 9" x 12", $20-35.

"The Tracks Of My Tears" – Smokey Robinson & The Miracles. This was a hit for The Miracles in 1965. This 1967 sheet music is a later printing from Johnny Rivers' release of the same song. 9" x 12", $10-15.

"Going To A Go-Go" – The Miracles. This 1966 sheet music has a photo that shows the group in matching tuxedo shirts. The song is from the album of the same name. 9" x 12", $20-40.

"The Bird Is the Word" – The Rivingtons. Early 1960s R&B tune. Printed in April of 1963. 8.5" x 11", rare, $60-75.

"Unchained Melody" – The Righteous Brothers. Credited to The Righteous Brothers but only one member of the duo, Bob Hatfield, is heard on the song. It gained popularity again in 1990 as part of the movie *Ghost*. 9" x 12", $30-40.

"My Guy" (Australia) – Mary Wells. Written by William "Smokey" Robinson of The Miracles. He also wrote "My Girl" for The Temptations. The U.S. version uses the same layout with a red title and border. 8.5" x 11", $15-20.

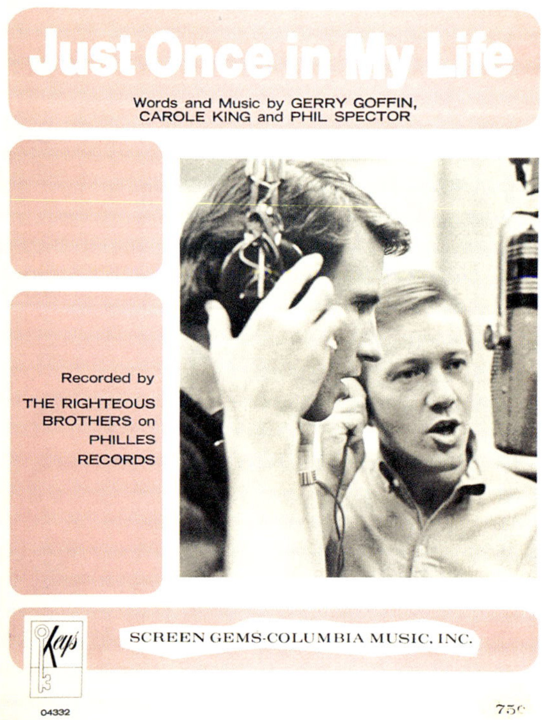


"Just Once in My Life" – The Righteous Brothers. Nice shot of the duo in the recording studio. Printed in April of 1965. 8.5" x 11", $15-25.

"A Man Without a Dream" – The Righteous Brothers. The layout for this sheet was used frequently for different artists. This was printed in November of 1966. 8.5" x 11", $15-25.

"Soul & Inspiration" (U.K. and U.S.) – The Righteous Brothers. Two versions of the sheet music for this very famous 1966 song—one from each side of the Atlantic. Both 8.5" x 11", U.K. $15-25; U.S. $30-45.

"You've Lost That Lovin' Feelin'" – The Righteous Brothers. Same photo as used on "Just Once In My Life." This particular printing is from February of 1965. 8.5" x 11", $25-40.

"The Letter" – The Box Tops. The photo shown here was commonly used on sheet music from The Box Tops. This song from 1967 was their biggest hit 9" x 12", $20-35.

"Respect" (U.K.) – Aretha Franklin. Beautiful photo of a young Aretha. This song was a chart topper for her in 1967. 8.5" x 11", $15-25.

"My Boy Lollipop" (U.K.) – Millie. Known as Millie Small in the United States, she was listed as only Millie on this U.K. release. 8.5" x 11", $15-25.

"Soul Deep" – The Box Tops. The original selling price of this 1969 sheet was 85¢, not 95¢ as is rubber stamped on the cover. 9" x 12", $25-35.

"Cry Like a Baby" – The Box Tops. The cover shows a tear drawn under the word "cry" for emphasis. This sheet was printed in April of 1968. 8.5" x 11", $30-40.

"Choo Choo Train" – The Box Tops. This May 1968 release shows the band dressed in flower printed, psychedelic, Nehru styled shirts. 8.5" x 11", $15-25.

"Wonderful! Wonderful!" – The Tymes. Second hit for The Tymes; the first was "So Much In Love." This sheet music has notations for both guitar and ukulele. 9" x 12", $30-45.

"Come On Over to My Place" – The Drifters. The Drifters had the majority of their hits in the late 1950s and early 1960s. This 1965 release gave them only minor success. 8.5" x 11", $30-45.

"I Could Never Love Another (After Loving You)" – The Temptations. A song that tells the oft-told tale of true love and a broken heart. 9" x 12", $20-40.

The Temptations were hugely successful Motown recording artists from Detroit. They were signed to Motown in 1961, but didn't have their first major hit until 1964. After lead singer David Ruffin left in 1968, the group took off in a different direction by experimenting with socially conscious lyrics and modern recording techniques. This helped define the sound known as psychedelic soul. The following six pieces of sheet music were all from this time in the late 1960s and utilize only two different photos between them. The graphics and drawings that surround the pictures give each sheet its own personality.

"Cloud Nine" – The Temptations. Song from 1968 about illegal drug use. 9" x 12", $20-35.

"I Can't Get Next To You" – The Temptations. Chart topper from August of 1969. 9" x 12", $20-35.

"(Loneliness Made Me Realize) It's You That I Need" – The Temptations. From the 1967 album *With a Lot O' Soul*. 9" x 12", $20-35.

"You're My Everything" – The Temptations. This song reached its highest chart position, number six, in July of 1967. 9" x 12", $20-35.

"A Lovers Concerto" (Australia) – The Toys. This trio of lovely ladies hailed from Jamaica, New York. The song is from 1965. 8.5" x 11", $15-20.

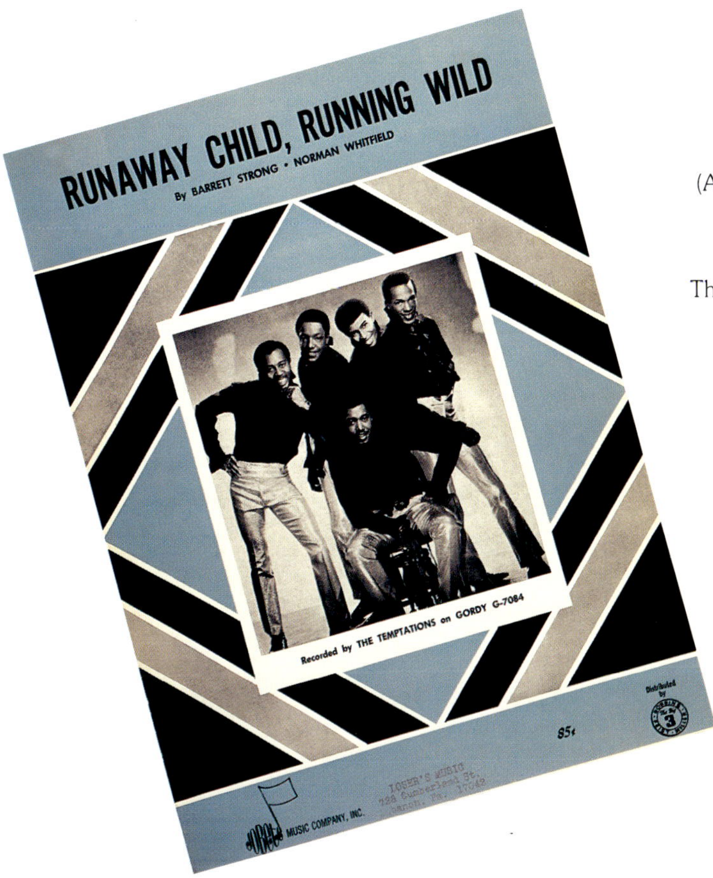


"Runaway Child, Running Wild" – The Temptations. In this song, a runaway teenager finds out he may have been better off staying at home. 9" x 12", $20-35.

The Four Tops had a string of unsuccessful songs until signing with Motown in 1963. Eventually they became one of that label's most prosperous groups. The sheet music for two of their songs released in 1966 show the same photo and layout with slightly different backgrounds. Motown's hit songwriting team of Holland, Dozier, and Holland wrote each of the five songs shown here.

"It's the Same Old Song" – The Four Tops. The sheet music for this tune about lost love was printed in August of 1965. 8.5" x 11", $35-45.

"Standing in the Shadows Of Love" – The Four Tops. This song hit the charts in December of 1966. It was featured on the August 1967 album *Four Tops Reach Out*. 9" x 12", $20-35.

"I Can't Help Myself" – The Four Tops. The very first number one hit on the pop charts for this Detroit based group. 8.5" x 11", $40-50.

"Baby I Need Your Loving" – The Four Tops. This song was the first chart hit for The Four Tops in 1964, but this piece of sheet music was printed in 1967 when Johnny Rivers released his cover version. 9" x 12", $10-15.

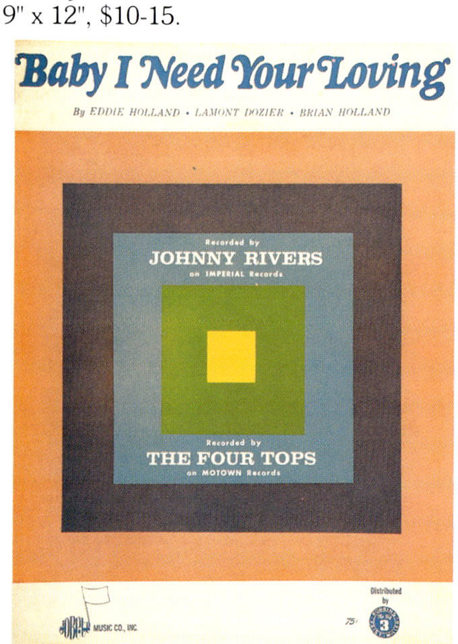

"Reach Out I'll Be There" – The Four Tops. Number one song for The Four Tops in 1966. This is one of the most common sheet music releases for this group. 9" x 12", $20-30.

"Gimme Little Sign" – Brenton Wood. From October of 1967, this sheet music has been printed a little off center, which will lower the value. 8.5" x 11", $20-30.

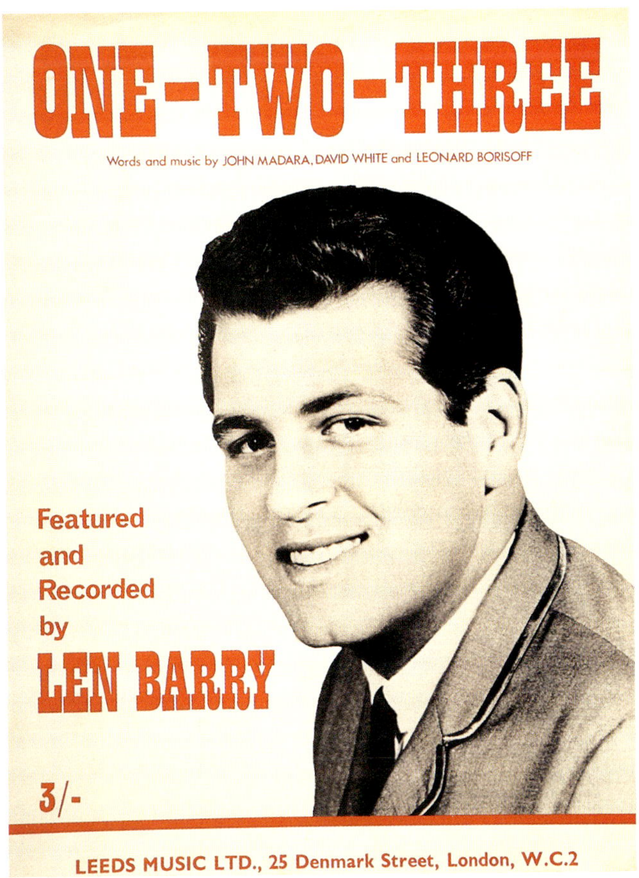


"One-Two-Three" (U.K.) – Len Barry. Barry, the former lead singer of The Dovells, took this song to number two in the U.S. and number three in Britain in 1965. 8.5" x 11", $15-20.

"Do You Know the Way to San Jose" – Dionne Warwick. A seductive photo of Warwick graces the cover of this 1968 song. 9" x 12", $15-20.

"For Once in My Life" – Stevie Wonder. Number two hit on both the pop and R&B charts in 1968. 9" x 12", $15-25.

"My Cherie Amour" – Stevie Wonder. Co-written by Wonder himself, this song appeared on the 1969 album of the same name. 9" x 12", $15-25.

"Uptight (Everything's Alright)" – Stevie Wonder. First top five hit after dropping the "Little" from his name. 9" x 12", $25-35.

Chapter Six

# "Catch Us If You Can"

## The British Invasion

After The Beatles appeared on *The Ed Sullivan Show* in February of 1964 and basically conquered America, other English bands were quick to follow them, sending much of their music across the Atlantic. The resulting invasion lasted most of the remainder of the decade. Americans loved the new sound and group after group made their impression on the U.S. market. Between 1964 and 1966, the British bands dominated the American charts as well as the charts in the United Kingdom.[4]

Since many of these English bands had success in both America and at home, there are a myriad of songs that had sheet music printed for the same title in both countries. There are also a number of songs that never had U.S. sheet music printed for them, perhaps because the song was early in the band's career or maybe just not released in the States.

Certain bands from this style can be very popular with collectors, with values for sheet music corresponding to that interest. However, the best part about sheet music from the British Invasion is the joy of discovering all the unknown and obscure sheets from other countries.

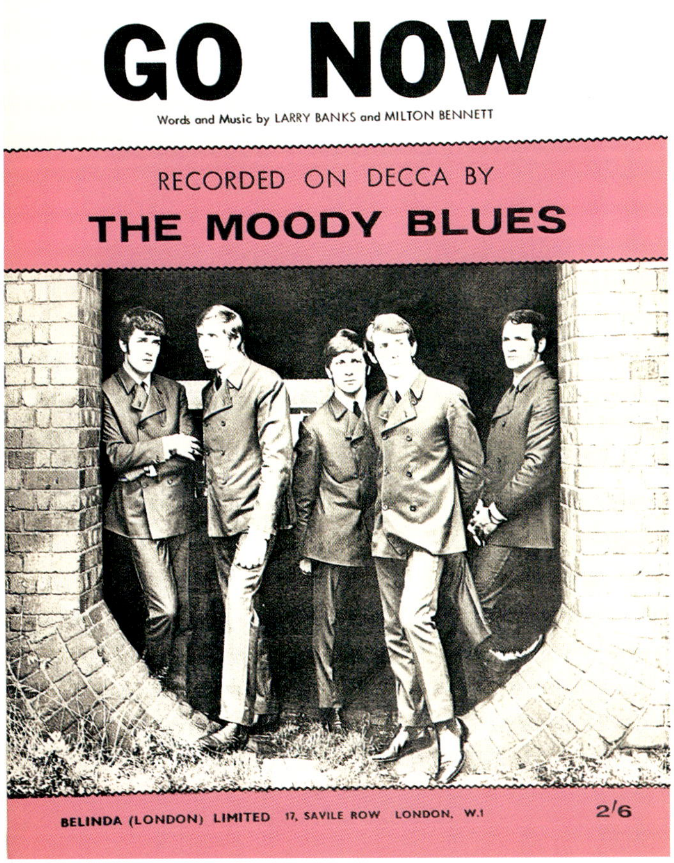


"Go Now" (U.K.) – The Moody Blues. First sheet music printed for The Moody Blues. Reached number ten on the U.S. pop charts and number one on the British charts. 8.5" x 11", $20-30.

"Itchycoo Park" – The Small Faces. Biggest hit for The Small Faces, climbing as high as number sixteen on the U.S. pop charts. Printed in February of 1968. 8.5" x 11", $10-20.

"Don't Let the Sun Catch You Crying" – Gerry & The Pacemakers. Gerry Marsden, lead singer of The Pacemakers and writer of this song, sports a cheeky grin on the cover of this 1964 sheet. 8.5" x 11", $15-25.

"Don't Let Me Be Misunderstood" (U.K.) – The Animals. 1965 number three song on the British charts. The name of the band is written as though it has fur on it, the way an animal would. 8.5" x 11", $20-30.

Close up photo of the group's name from the "Don't Let Me Be Misunderstood" sheet music. The extra lines give the words an animal-like appearance.

"Ferry Cross the Mersey" (U.K.) – Gerry & The Pacemakers. Title song from the 1964 British film of the same name. The cover shows pictures from the film. 8.5" x 11", $10-20.

"Don't Bring Me Down" – The Animals. Great Sixties styled cover with a shot of the band in concert with orange and black graphics. 8.5" x 11", $20-40.

"House of the Rising Sun" – The Animals. Biggest hit of The Animals' career, this song went to number one in both Britain and the United States. 8.5" x 11", $30-45.

"House Of the Rising Sun" (Sweden) – The Animals. This song was a huge international hit, with sheet music being printed for it in at least four different countries: the United States, The United Kingdom, Australia, and Sweden—where this sheet is from. The lyrics are printed in English only. 8.75" x 12", very rare, $15-25.

"We've Gotta Get Out of This Place" (U.K.) – The Animals. 1965 tune about life in a go-nowhere town that became an anthem for the Vietnam era. 8.5" x 11", $20-35.

"You've Got Your Troubles" – The Fortunes. The Fortunes had a top ten hit with this song on both the British and U.S. charts in 1965. 9" x 12", $15-25.

"I'm a Man" – The Spencer Davis Group. Rare sheet music that features Steve Winwood before he left to form the band Traffic. 9" x 12", $50-65.

"Gimme Some Loving" – The Spencer Davis Group. Number seven tune from 1966. The sheet shown here was hand signed for the author by Spencer Davis at the Westbury Music Fair on Long Island, New York on July 14, 2001. 9" x 12", value without autograph $20-40.

"Even the Bad Times Are Good" (U.K.) – The Tremeloes. The cover of this 1967 tune shows the band performing on a British television show. This sheet music is quite common and can be found frequently on Internet auctions. 8.5" x 11", $10-15.

"Here Comes My Baby" (U.K.) – The Tremeloes. First song to chart for this band in the United Kingdom. The song was written by Cat Stevens. 8.5" x 11", $15-20.

"Silence Is Golden" (U.K. and U.S.) – The Tremeloes. Popular ballad that rose to number one on the British charts and number eleven in the U.S. in 1967. Both sheets have a yellow-gold coloring to them that refers to the title. U.K. 8.5" x 11", $15-20; U.S. 9" x 12", $20-25.

"A Little Loving" (U.K.) – The Fourmost. This sheet music from the United Kingdom is very unusual as it is printed in full color. U.K. sheet music from the 1960s was normally only printed in black and white with one other color. 8.5" x 11", $15-20.

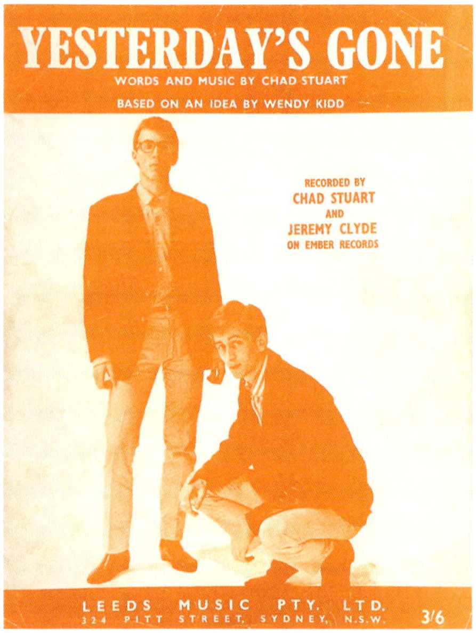


"Yesterday's Gone" (Australia) – Chad & Jeremy. First single from this group. This sheet refers to the duo by their full names, Chad Stuart and Jeremy Clyde, rather than simply Chad & Jeremy, as they are known in the United States. 8.5" x 11", $10-15.

"Downtown" (U.K.) – Petula Clark. Petula had many hits in Britain before this 1964 release, but this was her first tune to chart in the United States, where it went all the way to number one. 8.5" x 11", $10-15.

"I Know a Place" (Australia) – Petula Clark. This 1965 song was written about The Cavern, the underground Liverpool club that The Beatles made famous. 8.5" x 11", $15-25.

"Don't Sleep in the Subway" – Petula Clark. This common sheet has a truly pretty cover showing Petula in her "poor boy" cap. 9" x 12", $15-25.

"Time of the Season" – The Zombies. This 1967 song was released in the U.S. after the band had already broken up. 9" x 12", $15-30.

"She's Not There" (Australia) – The Zombies. This sheet music from "down under" shows the original selling price written in pounds sterling rather than Australian dollars. The song was this band's biggest American hit, going all the way to number two in 1964. 8.5" x 11", $15-25.

"Do The Freddie" – Freddie & The Dreamers. This song also had a dance to go along with it. The silly kicks and arm movements became something of a trademark for the band and their lead singer. Instructions on how to do "The Freddie" can be found on the back cover. 8.5" x 11", $15-25.

"Tell Her No" – The Zombies. This top ten hit has the dubious distinction of using the word "no" over 60 times. Printed in January of 1965. 8.5" x 11", $30-45.

Back cover of "Do The Freddie," with simple pictures that attempt to explain how to do this dance. If you've ever actually done "The Freddie," however, these pictures look nothing like it.

Surly British exports The Rolling Stones took America by storm in 1965 with a trio of number one hits: "The Last Time," "(I Can't Get No) Satisfaction," and "Get Off Of My Cloud." Sheet music from the Stones is always sought after, particularly the U.S. version of "Not Fade Away," which was the first Rolling Stones sheet music to be printed in America. It is interesting to note that sheet music printings that show Keith Richards' last name as "Richard" are not errors. He did indeed drop the "s" for a few years.

"I'm Telling You Now" – Freddie & The Dreamers. Biggest hit for Freddie & The Dreamers that went all the way to number one in the United States in 1965, two years after it went to number two in Britain. 9" x 12", $10-20.

"You Were Made For Me" (U.K.) – Freddie & The Dreamers. Casual shot of the band joking around in front of Buckingham Palace. 8.5" x 11", $10-15.

"Get Off of My Cloud" (U.K.) – The Rolling Stones. Given the unusual band names of the day, this sheet music clears the confusion by pointing out which is the singer and which is the song. The sheet is the same on both the front and back. 8.5" x 11", $25-40.

"Get Off of My Cloud" – The Rolling Stones. The song went to number one in 1965; this sheet music was printed in December of that year. 8.5" x 11", $30-50.

"You Were Made For Me" – Freddie & The Dreamers. This sheet music shows the name Freddie misspelled with a "y" instead of an "ie" in 1965. 9" x 12", $10-15.

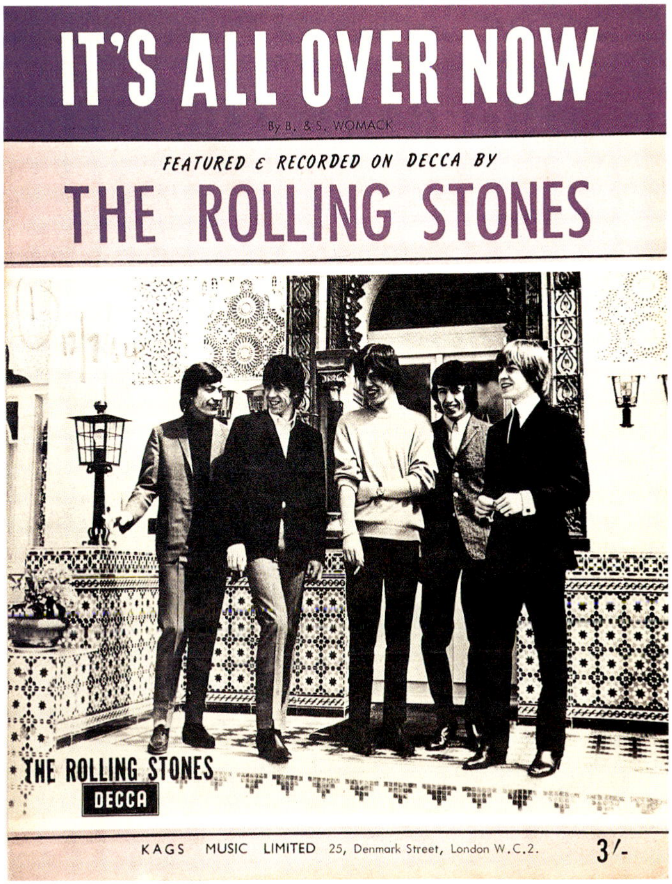


"It's All Over Now" (U.K.) – The Rolling Stones. Uncommon sheet for a song that did much better in Britain (number one) than it did in the U.S., where it only went to number twenty-six. 8.5" x 11", $20-40.

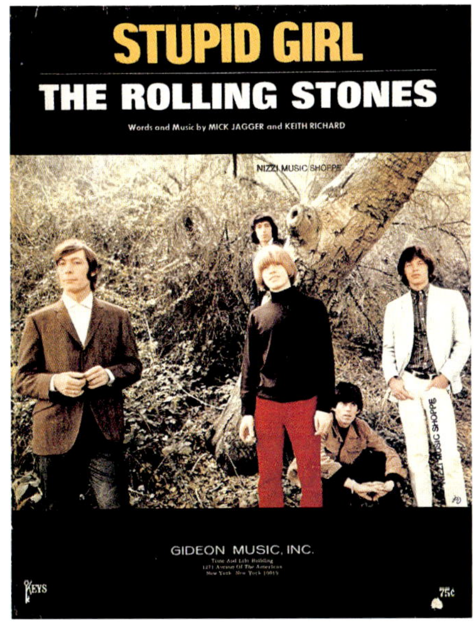


"Stupid Girl" – The Rolling Stones. Lesser-known song for a very well known band. "Paint It, Black" uses the same cover. 8.5" x 11", $20-30.

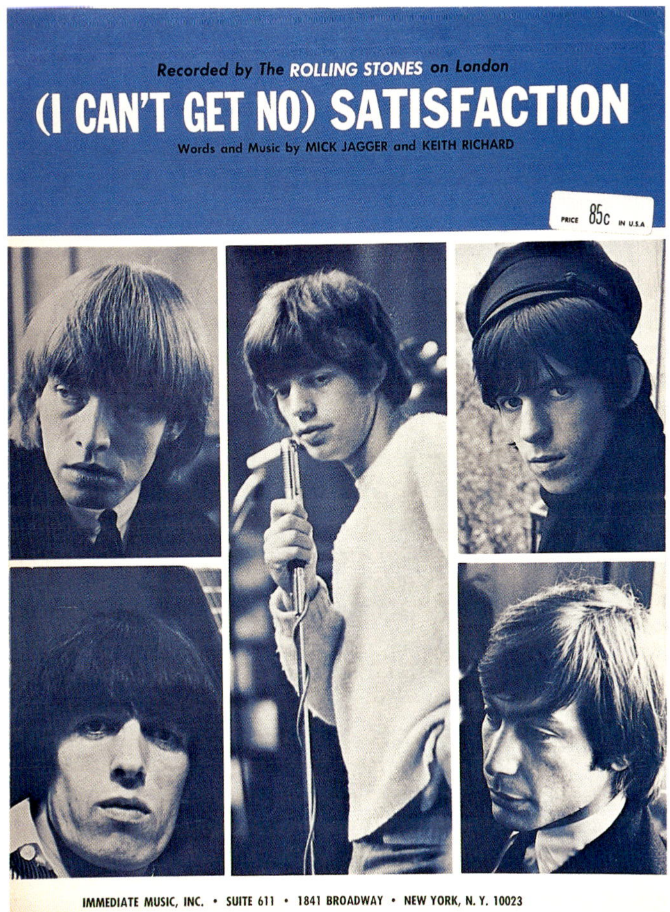


"(I Can't Get No) Satisfaction" – The Rolling Stones. This is the second, more common, printing of the sheet music for this song. The first uses the same cover only in shades of red and has an original selling price of only 60¢. 9" x 12", $30-50.

"Not Fade Away" – The Rolling Stones. The rarest sheet music printed for The Rolling Stones in the United States. This song was their first release in America back in 1964 and it only charted as high as number forty-eight. Since they were a new group in America and the single didn't perform well, few copies of the sheet music were sold. 9" x 12", $150-175.

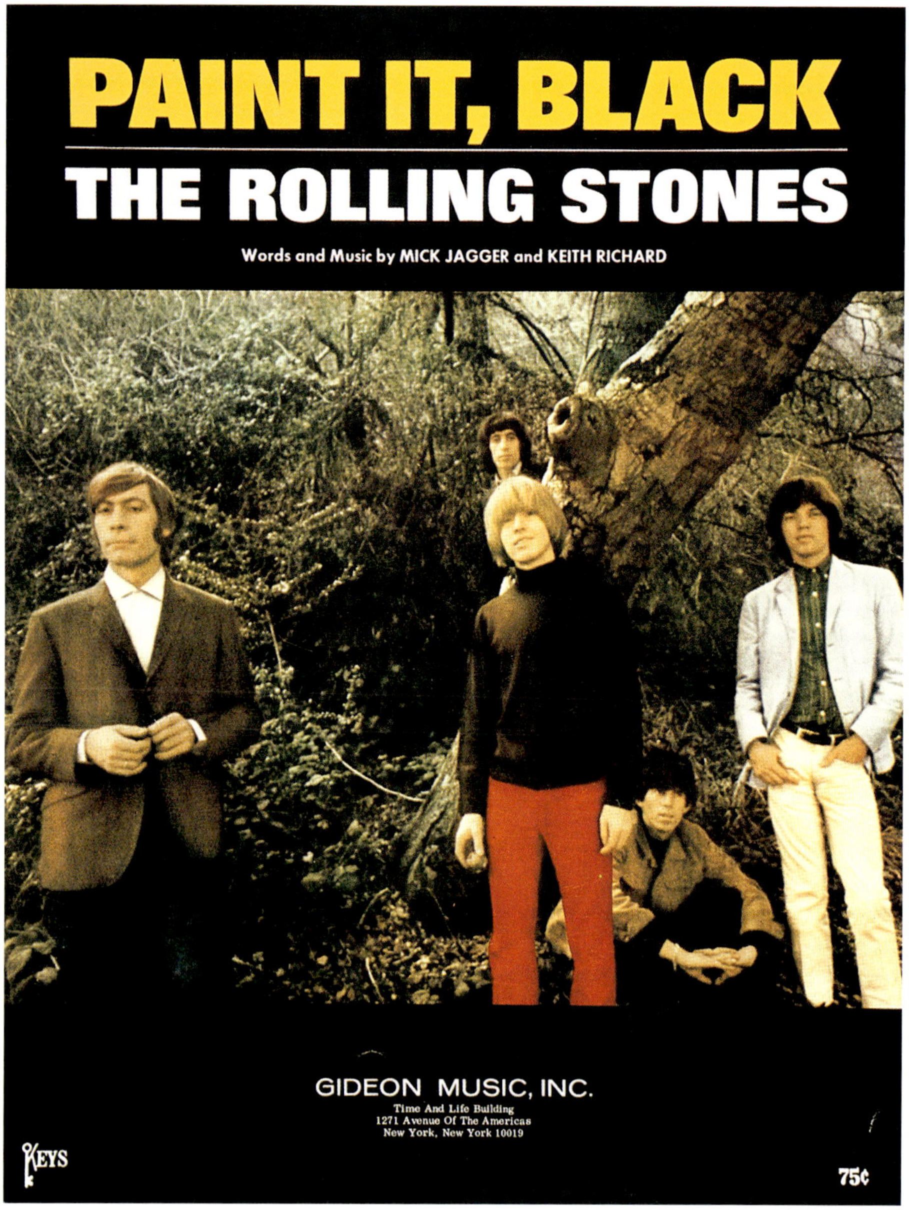


"Paint It, Black" – The Rolling Stones. Huge song for the Stones that rose to number one on both the American and British charts. 8.5" x 11", $25-40.

"Jumpin' Jack Flash" (Australia) – The Rolling Stones. Devilish photo of the group playing around with various studio props. The same cover was used on the U.K. printing. 8.5" x 11", $15-20.

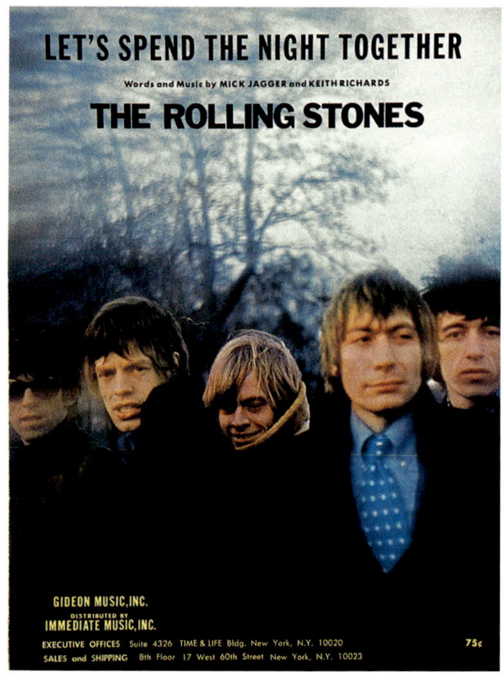


"Let's Spend the Night Together" – The Rolling Stones. This song was the flip side to "Ruby Tuesday." The sheet music to both songs uses the same cover photo. 9" x 12", $25-35.

"Is This What I Get For Loving You?" – Marianne Faithfull. Ms. Faithfull is probably better known for her relationship with Mick Jagger than her recording career. This sheet was printed in April of 1967. 8.5" x 11", $10-15.

"Bend It!" (U.K.) – Dave Dee, Dozy, Beaky, Mick & Tich. This number two British single from 1966 had its very own dance to go with it. Instructions are included as a separate pull out sheet. 8.5" x 11", $10-15.

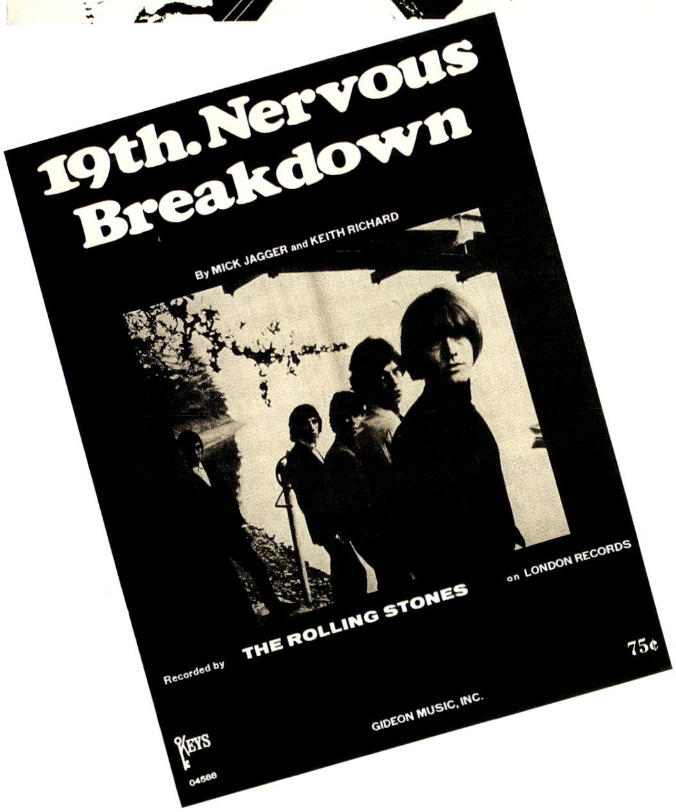


"19th Nervous Breakdown" (U.K. and U.S.) – The Rolling Stones. Two simple but interesting sheets for this 1966 song that charted as high as number two in both America and Britain. The U.K. sheet has the same photo on both sides. The U.S. sheet was printed in February 1966. Both 8.5" x 11", U.K. $20-30; U.S. $25-40.

Pull out instructions on how to do The Bend, included with the "Bend It!" sheet music.

"Zabadak" (U.K.) – Dave Dee, Dozy, Beaky, Mick & Tich. Cover of this 1967 sheet music is adorned not only with the floating heads of the band members, but also the song's nonsense words written in the sand. 8.5" x 11", $10-15.

"World Without Love" – Peter & Gordon. Peter Asher and Gordon Waller recorded this Lennon-McCartney tune in 1964. Peter had regular access to The Beatles, as his sister Jane was dating Paul McCartney. 8.5" x 11", $15-30.

"Woman" (Australia) – Peter & Gordon. This 1966 song was written by Bernard Webb, a pseudonym for Paul McCartney. 8.5" x 11", $10-20.

"That's the Way" (U.K.) – The Honeycombs. The band was named for their female drummer, Ann "Honey" Lantree. They are better known in America for their song "Have I the Right." 8.5" x 11", $7-12.

"Lady Godiva" (Australia and U.S.) – Peter & Gordon. While the U.S. version uses a standard cover with a common photo, the Australian sheet music shows a much more interesting cover. It includes an art-nouveau styled title and a photo of Peter & Gordon with a young girl "dressed" as Lady Godiva herself. Australia 8.5" x 11", $15-20; U.S. 9" x 12", $10-15.

"Do Wah Diddy Diddy" – Manfred Mann. Very familiar song that went to number one in 1964. 9" x 12", $20-35.

"Sweet Pea" (U.K.) – Manfred Mann. Instrumental version of Tommy Roe's 1966 top ten hit. There is no U.S. sheet music for this tune. 8.5" x 11", $10-15.

"Quinn the Eskimo (Mighty Quinn)" (U.K.) – Manfred Mann. This photo seems to have caught the band off guard. The title of this 1968 tune is reversed from the U.S. version. 8.5" x 11", $15-20.

"Sha La La" (U.K.) – Manfred Mann. 1964 song that rose to number three on the British charts and number twelve on the U.S. charts. 8.5" x 11", $10-20.

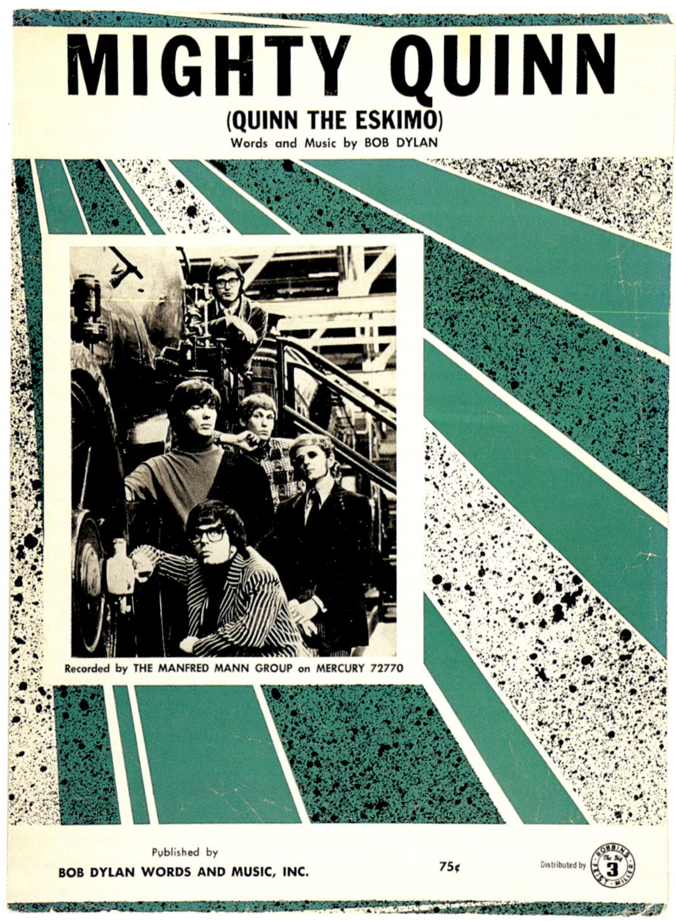


"Mighty Quinn (Quinn the Eskimo)" – Manfred Mann. Written by Bob Dylan, this song climbed to number ten in the United States. 9" x 12", $10-15.

"I Stand Accused" (U.K.) – The Mersey Beats. Last single released by the band in 1966; they split up shortly after. The title of this song was drawn by hand. 8.5" x 11", $10-15.

"Do You Want To Know a Secret?" (U.K.) – Billy J. Kramer & The Dakotas. Kramer and his group were able to take this song, written by John Lennon and Paul McCartney, to number two in Britain in 1963. 8.5" x 11", $15-20.

"Little Children" (U.K.) – Billy J. Kramer & The Dakotas. This 1964 song was a number one single for Kramer and The Dakotas. 8.5" x 11", $10-15.

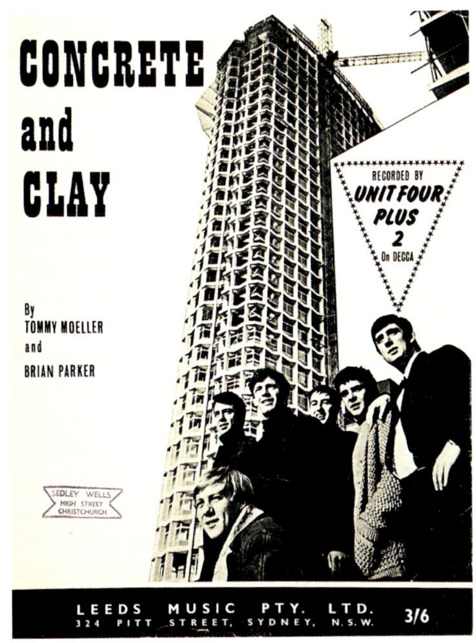


"Concrete and Clay" (Australia) – Unit Four Plus 2. The six-man group had a hit with this song in 1965. 8.5" x 11", $10-15.

The Dave Clark Five was a successful beat group that played bright, memorable, danceable music that still permeates the airwaves today. Led by clever businessman Clark, the band managed to keep a lively career going on both sides of the Atlantic for many years. Their sheet music releases are numerable and a number of different titles can be found in the U.S., the U.K., and Australia as well.

"Because" – The Dave Clark Five. This is a U.S. only single for this British band. 8.5" x 11", $25-35.

"Catch Us If You Can" – The Dave Clark Five. This song is from the 1965 film, *Having a Wild Weekend*, which starred The Dave Clark Five. 8.5" x 11", $15-25.

"I Like It Like That" – The Dave Clark Five. Co-written by R&B legend Allen Toussaint. 8.5" x 11", $15-20.

"Can't You See That She's Mine" (U.K.) – The Dave Clark Five. Top ten song on both the U.S. and U.K. charts. 8.5" x 11", $10-20.

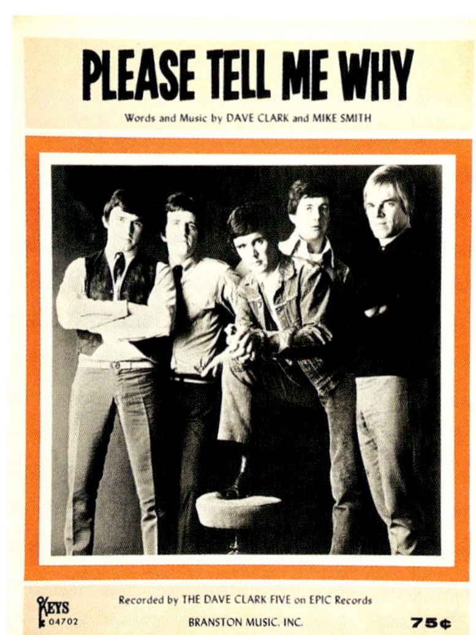


"Please Tell Me Why" – The Dave Clark Five. Standard cover layout is used on this 1966 song. 8.5" x 11", $10-20.

"Glad All Over" – The Dave Clark Five. Two different versions of the U.S. sheet music for this song. The version with the pale blue background was printed in February 1964, a month earlier than the other sheet. Both 8.5" x 11", $15-25.

"Bits and Pieces" (U.K.) – The Dave Clark Five. The cover photo shows drummer Clark posed behind his drums, but still the focal point of the picture. 8.5" x 11", $10-20.

"Winchester Cathedral" – Geoff Stephens' New Vaudeville Band. Extremely common sheet music for this 1966 number one song. 9" x 12", $7-12.

"Winchester Cathedral" (U.K.) – Geoff Stephens' New Vaudeville Band. Very popular song had at least two different sheet music printings in the United Kingdom. 8.5" x 11", $10-15.

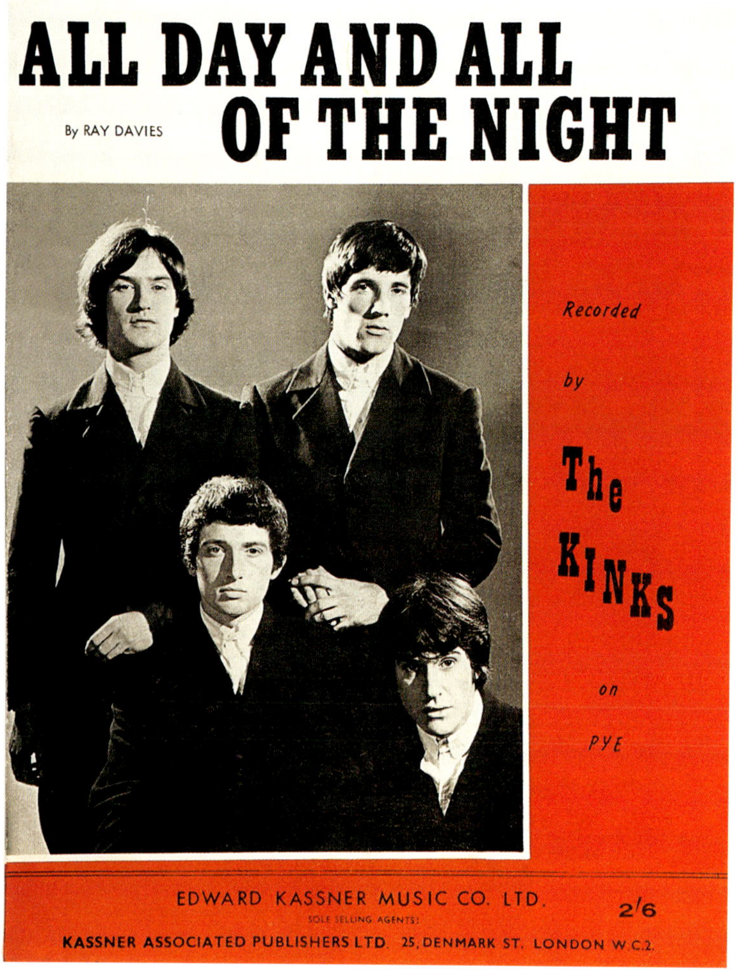


"All Day and All of the Night" (U.K.) – The Kinks. Standard U.K. cover layout was used on this 1964 sheet. 8.5" x 11", $15-30.

"Wonderboy" (Holland) – The Kinks. This mini sheet is from the Netherlands, for one of the lesser-known Kinks singles. While the cover is in Dutch, the lyrics are printed only in English. 6.5" x 9.25", $10-20.

"All Day & All Of the Night" – The Kinks. Fun photo of the band out hunting, with everyone pointing at the quarry except the dog. The cover of this sheet also notes the "Jan. 4 Chart." 8.5" x 11", $25-40.

"You Really Got Me" (U.K.) – The Kinks. Raw and edgy first hit for The Kinks. It was released before the band ever had an album recorded. 8.5" x 11", $20-35.

"Tobacco Road" (U.K.) – The Nashville Teens. Basically one-hit wonders in the U.S., they fared much better in their native England. The song was written by John D. Loudermilk. 8.5" x 11", $10-15.

"Tired of Waiting For You" – The Kinks. This ballad was the band's third single to hit the top ten in America; in Britain, it was the third to reach the top five. 9" x 12", $25-40.

"Why Not Tonight" (U.K.) – The Mojos. Unusual circular cover photo has each band member's name printed near his picture, a common practice for U.K. sheet music. 8.5" x 11", $10-15.

"Everything's Al'right" (U.K.) – The Mojos. The Mojos didn't exactly invade America; they are not well known in the states. This sheet is from 1964. 8.5" x 11", $10-15.

"Mrs. Brown You've Got a Lovely Daughter" (U.K.) – Herman's Hermits. Sweet tune made all the more charming by lead singer Peter Noone and his heavy British accent. 8.5" x 11", $15-20.

With their youthful good looks and quirky, catchy songs, Herman's Hermits became heartthrobs to countless young girls in the mid-Sixties. Their faces graced the cover of numerous teen magazines where their lead singer was often referred to as "Herman" even though his real name was Peter Noone. Although they did not compose music themselves, they managed to record songs from some of the top writers of the day, giving them a multitude of hits in Britain and America.

"Henry the VIII" – Herman's Hermits. This electrified version of an old English folk song went to number one in 1965. The cover proudly states the song is "from their second album *Herman's Hermits On Tour*." 9" x 12", $15-25.

"No Milk Today" (U.K.) – Herman's Hermits. This song about a broken heart hit the British charts in 1966 and the American charts in 1967. The cover photo doesn't appear on any of the band's other sheet music printings. 8.5" x 11", $10-20.

"I'm Into Something Good" (U.K. and U.S.) – Herman's Hermits. This was the first single released for the group in both Britain and America, where it rose to number one and number thirteen, respectively. Brill Building songwriters Gerry Goffin and Carole King are credited with writing the song. Both 8.5" x 11", U.K. $15-25; U.S. $20-30.

"This Door Swings Both Ways" – Herman's Hermits. Common cover layout was used on sheets for other bands, including "Wild Thing" by The Troggs. 9" x 12", $10-15.

"Don't Go Out Into the Rain (You're Gonna Melt)" – Herman's Hermits. Adorable front cover combines a cute photo of the band with drawings of people walking in the rain. Printed in July of 1967. 8.5" x 11", $10-20.

"There's a Kind of Hush (All Over the World)" – Herman's Hermits. Co-written by Geoff Stephens, whose New Vaudeville Band also recorded the song. 9" x 12", $10-15.

"The Hippy Hippy Shake" (U.K.) – The Swinging Blue Jeans. Written and recorded by Latino singer Chan Romero in 1959, it was released by The Swinging Blue Jeans in 1964 where it traveled to number two on the British charts. 8.5" x 11", $10-20.

"Dandy" (U.K.) – Herman's Hermits. While the most well known version of this song is by Herman's Hermits, it was also recorded by The Rocking Vickers and The Kinks, whose lead singer, Ray Davies, wrote the words and music. 8.5" x 11", $10-15.

"Bumble Bee" – The Searchers. The name of this band was allegedly taken from the 1956 John Wayne western, *The Searchers*. This sheet music was printed in April of 1965. 8.5" x 11", $15-25.

"Sugar & Spice" (U.K.) – The Searchers. Striking red cover sets apart this number two British single. 8.5" x 11", $10-15.

"Mystic Eyes" – Them. 1965 tune written by lead vocalist, Van Morrison. This sheet was printed in December of that year. 8.5" x 11", $25-40.

"Needles & Pins" – The Searchers. This 1964 song was co-written by Sonny Bono. Interestingly, although the song was made famous by a male group, the lyrics read as if it were being sung by a woman. 9" x 12", $15-30.

While starting their career singing R&B covers, The Hollies eventually began to write their own material, which led to memorable songs such as "Carrie Ann," "On a Carousel," and "Stop, Stop, Stop." The team of Allan Clarke, Tony Hicks, and Graham Nash wrote many of the band's early songs and published them under the pseudonym of L. Ransford. The Hollies were successful in the United Kingdom for some time before they made a splash in America, so by acquiring U.K. printings, a collector can find many rare songs not seen on sheet music in the U.S.

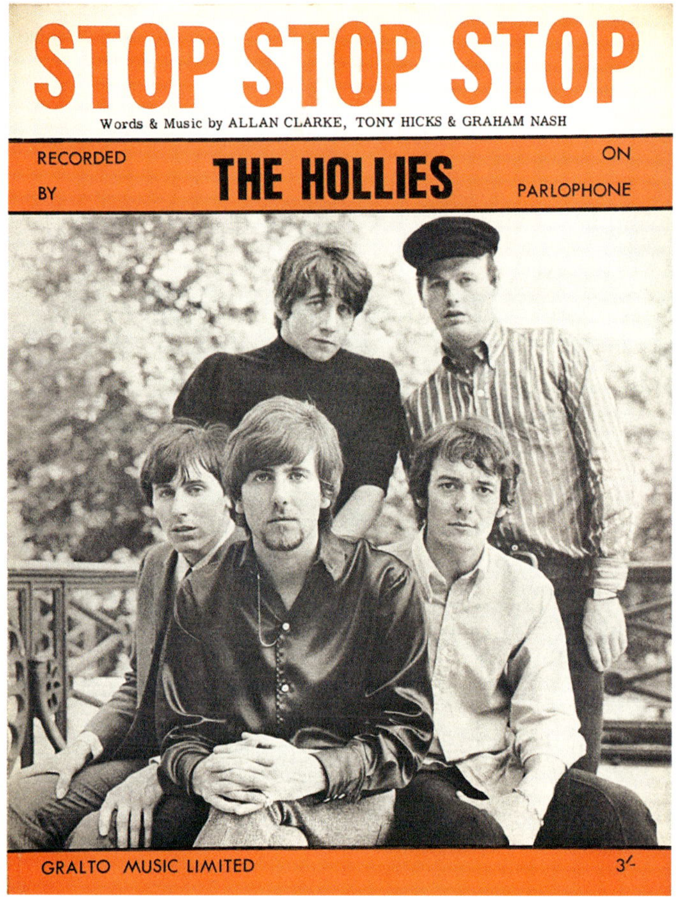


"Stop, Stop, Stop" (U.K.) – The Hollies. Number two song for The Hollies on the British charts in 1966. The sheet uses a standard U.K. layout with a black and white photo and colored bands on the top and bottom. 8.5" x 11", $10-20.

"Carrie Ann" – The Hollies. This song became a top ten hit for the band in both America and Britain in 1967. 9" x 12", $20-30.

"On a Carousel" – The Hollies. Great guitar work at the beginning of this 1967 song gives the listener the up and down feeling of actually being on a carousel. Lyrically, the sheet music mixes up the verses, putting what is obviously the fourth and last verse, before the third. 8.5" x 11", $20-30.

"Stop, Stop, Stop" – The Hollies. The exotic, Middle-Eastern melody of this song didn't stop the designers of this sheet music cover from styling it in traditional U.S. fashion with a giant octagonal stop sign. 8.5" x 11", $20-30.

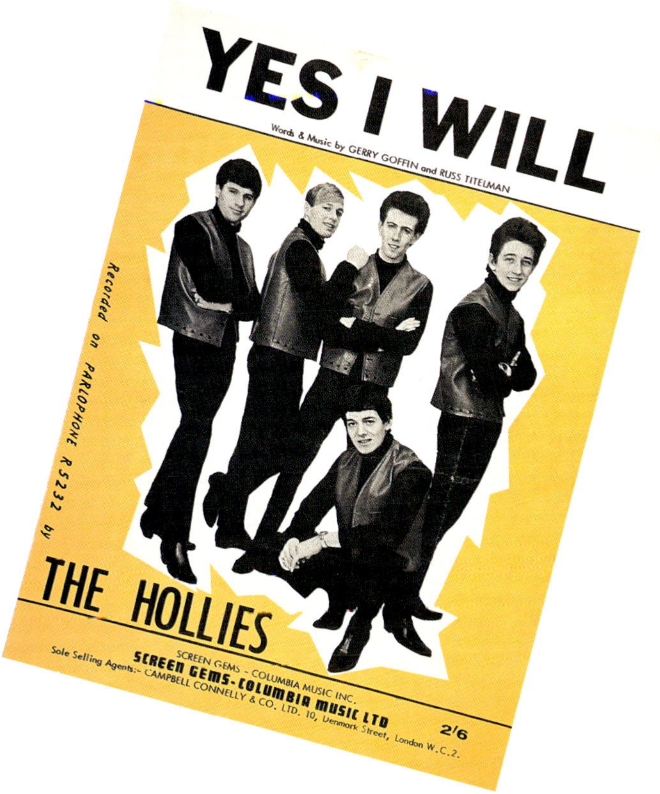


"Yes I Will" (U.K.) – The Hollies. This early U.K. only sheet was issued in 1965. 8.5" x 11", $10-15.

"We're Through" (U.K.) – The Hollies. Great, early U.K. sheet. There was no U.S. printing of this song. Written by members of the band under the name L. Ransford. 8.5" x 11", $20-35.

"Bus Stop" (U.K.) – The Hollies. The band name on this 1966 sheet is given special treatment with a handwritten design. The exact same cover was used on the Australian printing of this song. 8.5" x 11", $15-20.

"Bus Stop" – The Hollies. Cute but simple hand drawn cover depicting the hero and heroine of the song under the umbrella that started their romance. 9" x 12", $15-20.

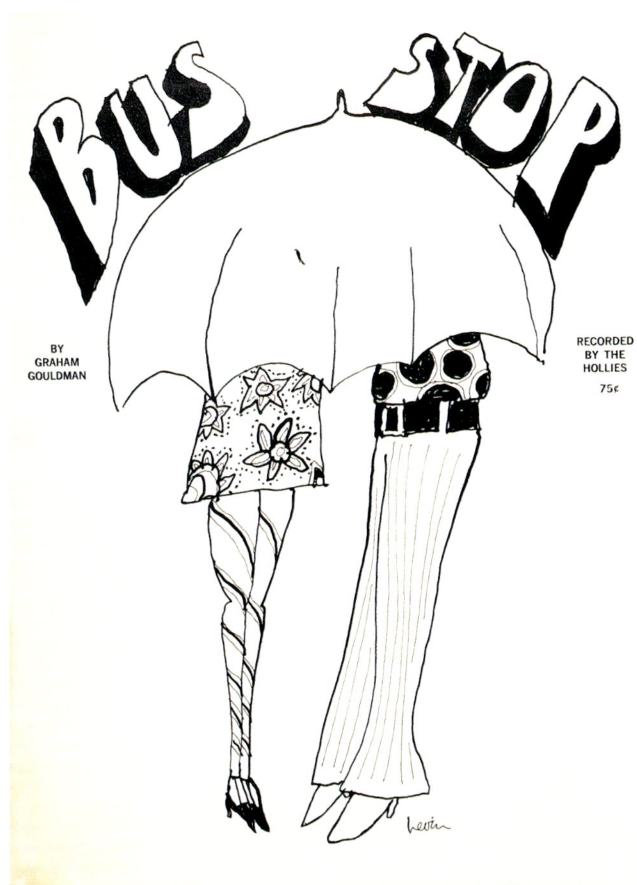

"All Day" (U.K.) – The Shadows. Also known as Cliff Richard's backing band, The Shadows were artists in their own right. This lesser-known instrumental release is from 1962. 8.5" x 11", $10-20.

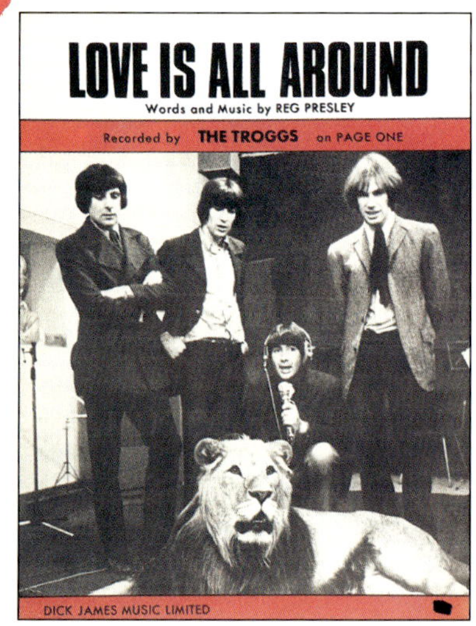


"Love Is All Around" (U.S. and U.K.) – The Troggs. Both sheets shown here are printed with covers unique to the places they are from. The U.K. sheet shows the band in the studio with a new exotic "friend." The U.S. sheet perfectly illustrates the song title with a heart that goes around the photo. Both 8.5" x 11", U.S. $15-30; U.K. $10-20.

Close up of The Shadows' logo shows the four band members in silhouette.

"36-24-36" (U.K.) – The Shadows. Although this is an instrumental song, the title gives the listener a good idea of what the composers were thinking about when it was written. 8.5" x 11", $10-20.

"I Can't Control Myself" – The Troggs. Reg Presley, lead singer, is the composer of this song. Reg took his famous last name from Elvis himself. 8.5" x 11", $15-25.

"Babababa-ba" (Italy) – The Troggs. Unusual Italian mini sheet music has The Troggs on one side and an Italian solo artist on the other. The song is better known as "With a Girl Like You." The accompanying lyrics have been translated into Italian. 6.75" x 9.5", very rare, $10-20.

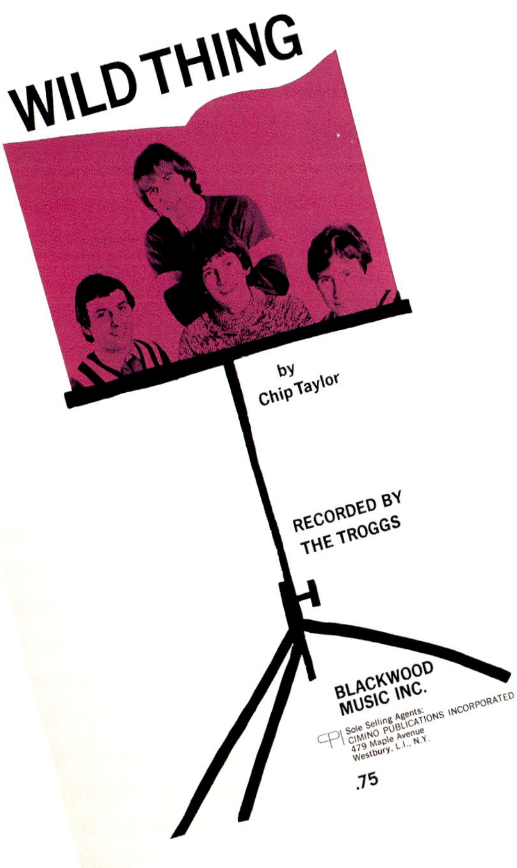


"Wild Thing" – The Troggs. Unfortunately common cover styling was used on this classic song. It rose to number one in 1966, putting The Troggs on the musical map. 9" x 12", $25-40.

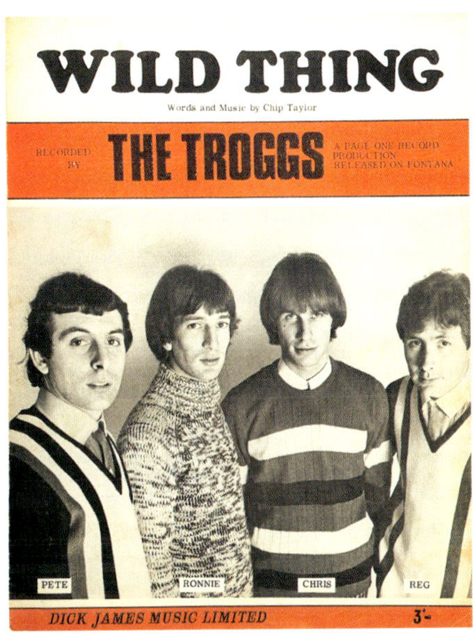


"Wild Thing" (U.K.) – The Troggs. The band's first release to chart in Britain (it went as high as number two), this song started a string of four top ten hits in their home country. 8.5" x 11", $20-30.

"A Groovy Kind of Love" – The Mindbenders. The American sheet music does not do this song justice, as it was printed without a photo of the band. The song charted as high as number two in both the U.S. and Britain in 1966. 8.5" x 11", $10-20.

"The Game Of Love" – Wayne Fontana & The Mindbenders. The Mindbenders originally started out as Wayne Fontana's backing band. Together they recorded this song and took it all the way to number one on the U.S. charts in 1965. 9" x 12", $25-35.

"A Groovy Kind Of Love" (U.K.) – The Mindbenders. Nice cover photo of the band for this first single without Wayne Fontana. 8.5" x 11", $10-15.

Chapter Seven

# "Thank U Very Much"

## Bubblegum, Girl Groups, Novelty Songs, etc.

Here you will find "The Best of the Rest!"—various styles of music that haven't been granted a chapter of their own. The 1960s were a time of musical diversity and experimentation, with many different types of music being performed and enjoyed. While other styles of music perhaps had a more significant impact on the sound of the decade, the music shown here certainly cannot be overlooked and was often influential in its own right.

Whether it's bubblegum music with its lightweight, catchy melodies, novelty songs with their silly, unexpected lyrics, the romanticism of male vocals, or girl groups with their refined, yet innocent sound, all are important pieces of the 1960s musical puzzle. While doo-wop was fading out, soft rock was just beginning and country music was crossing over and combining with pop, the latter giving us yet another unique style. Each different sound made its own contribution to defining Sixties music as a whole.

Given the diverse grouping of sounds shown here, value and interest will vary greatly from one piece of sheet music to the next.

"Sugar, Sugar" – The Archies. This group existed in the studio only, with Ron Dante singing lead male vocals and Toni Wine handling the female voices. "Sugar, Sugar" was a number one song in 1969. The U.K. version was done with the colors black, white, and red, while the Australian version used those colors with a touch of green. 8.5" x 11", $15-30.

"Have You Heard" – The Duprees. New Jersey vocal quintet had a minor hit with this song in 1963. 8.5" x 11", $20-40.

"Delilah" – Tom Jones. 1968 song about a troubled man who kills his wife after she cheats on him. 9" x 12", $10-15.

"I'm a Fool" – Dino, Desi & Billy. While the boys did sing on their records, all the music was handled by studio musicians. This 1965 song managed to reach number seventeen on the pop charts. 9" x 12", $15-25.

"You're My Baby (And Don't You Forget It)" – The Vacels. This rare 1965 sheet was for the only charting single by this band. 8.5" x 11", $20-35.

"Not the Lovin' Kind" – Dino, Desi & Billy. This trio had some famous family members. Dino was Dean Martin's son and Desi was the son of Lucille Ball and Desi Arnaz. The third member was schoolmate Billy Hinsche. 9" x 12", $15-25.

"He's So Fine" – The Chiffons. The Chiffons' only number one song was this 1963 tune. 8.5" x 11", $30-45.

"Sweet Talkin' Guy" – The Chiffons. Lovely mid-Sixties photo of the girls from this New York based group. This sheet was printed in June of 1966. 8.5" x 11", $45-65.

"Poetry in Motion" – Johnny Tillotson. This was Tillotson's biggest hit, reaching number two in 1960. He is also responsible for singing the theme song to the TV show *Gidget* in 1965. 9" x 12", $25-40.

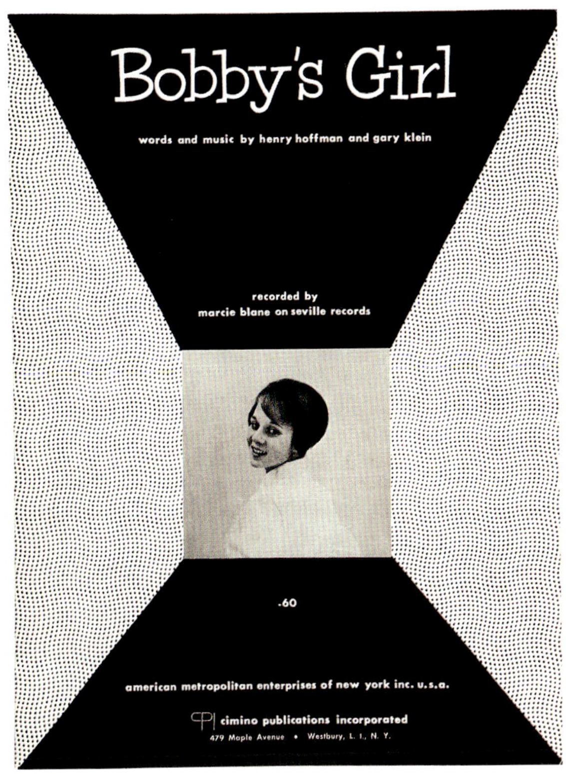


"Bobby's Girl" – Marcie Blane. While still a sought after sheet, it would be more desirable if the photo of Blane were larger. 9" x 12", $20-30.

"Honey" – Bobby Goldsboro. Second of two covers for this sheet music. The original, with a headshot of Goldsboro, was printed in April of 1968. This sheet is from July of 1969. 8.5" x 11", $10-15.

"Calendar Girl" – Neil Sedaka. Since the song mentions a calendar, that is exactly what is shown on the cover. Not surprisingly, this sheet music is from 1961. 9" x 12", $10-20.

"Happy Birthday Sweet Sixteen" (U.K.) – Neil Sedaka. A very debonair photo of Sedaka was used on this 1961 sheet. This same cover was used on the sheet music for "Breaking Up Is Hard To Do," except with a blue background. 8.5" x 11", $10-15.

"Soldier Boy" – The Shirelles. Popular girl group from New Jersey had a number one hit with this song in 1962. The sheet music cover is complete with soldier stars in the corners. 8.5" x 11", $20-35.

"Maybe Tomorrow" – The Iveys. Rare sheet music for The Iveys, the band that eventually became Badfinger. This sheet music was printed in February of 1969. 8.5" x 11", $20-35.

"Down in the Boondocks" – Billy Joe Royal. This "wrong side of the tracks" song was the biggest hit of Royal's career. There is also an alternate printing with an orange background. The sheet music was printed in September of 1965. 8.5" x 11", $15-25.

"It Hurts To Be In Love" – Gene Pitney. There are two different covers for the sheet music to this song. Although neither is very common, the other, which has a photo of Pitney, is more desirable. 8.5" x 11", $10-15.

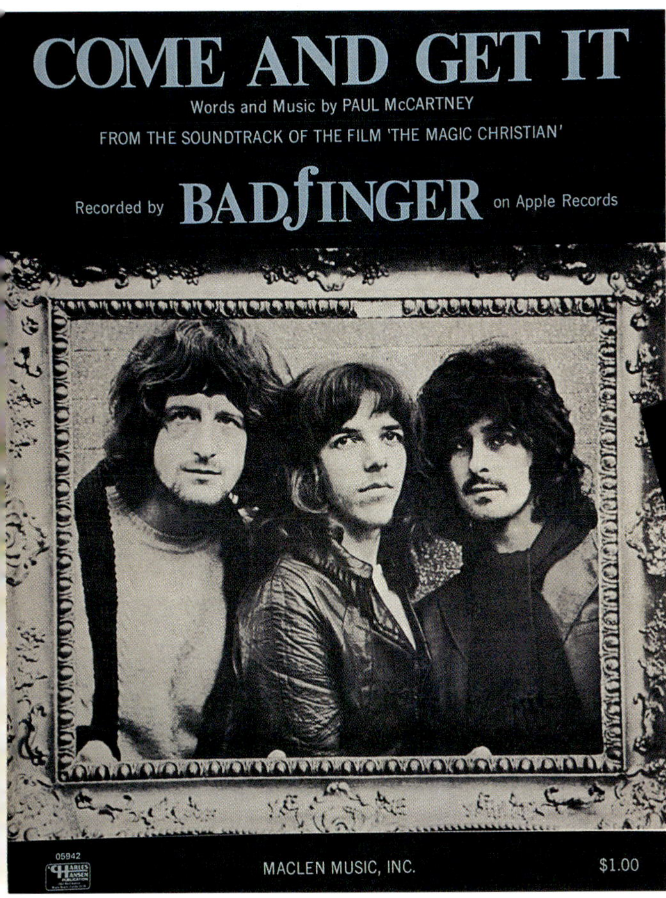


"Come and Get It" – Badfinger. Written by Paul McCartney and recorded on the Apple label, this song was featured in the movie *The Magic Christian*. It was the first hit for the band. 8.5" x 11", $20-40.

"It's My Party" – Lesley Gore. Lesley Gore is pretty as a picture on the cover of this 1963 sheet music for her only number one song. 9" x 12", $25-45.

"Sunshine, Lollipops and Rainbows" – Lesley Gore. Fantastic, colorful sheet for this 1965 tune. The cover perfectly captures the joyful nature of the song with the multicolored printing used for the title. 8.5" x 11", $20-35.

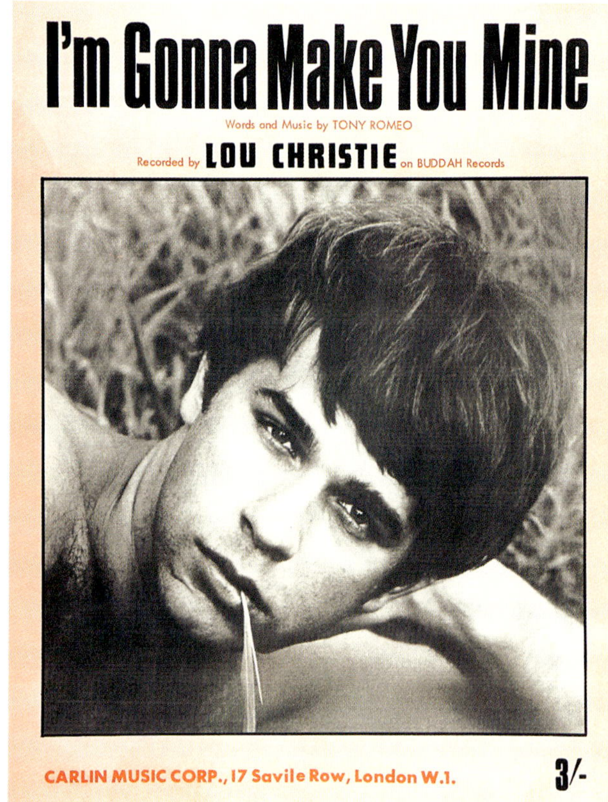


"I'm Gonna Make You Mine" (U.K.) – Lou Christie. This United Kingdom printing features a photo of Christie flashing a come-hither look. 8.5" x 11", $10-15.

"Lightnin' Strikes" – Lou Christie. Number one hit for Christie in February of 1966. This printing was issued in April of that year. 8.5" x 11", $15-30.

"Rhapsody in the Rain" – Lou Christie. This printing of the sheet music includes a lyric that was considered controversial at the time because it mentions "makin' out." Some of the first pressings of the 45rpm included the lyric, but it was removed from later pressings since radio stations were reluctant to play it as it was. 8.5" x 11", $15-30.

"Puppy Love" – Paul Anka. One of many singles for Anka throughout the 1950s, 1960s, and 1970s. This particular song rose to number two in 1960. 9" x 12", $7-12.

"I Wonder What She's Doing Tonight?" – Boyce & Hart. Echoing the question asked in the title of this 1968 song, the photo of the duo has been placed within a giant question mark. 8.5" x 11", $15-30.

Accomplished songwriters throughout the Sixties, Boyce and Hart composed a number of songs, most notably for The Monkees but for several other artists as well. During the middle of the decade, they began recording their own songs as a duo, with moderate success. They also appeared as themselves in episodes of two TV shows, *I Dream of Jeannie* and *Bewitched*.

"Out and About" – Boyce & Hart. Boyce and Hart are featured singing this song in an episode of *I Dream of Jeannie* entitled "Jeannie, the Hip Hippie." 8.5" x 11", $15-25.

"Tracy" (U.K.) – The Cuff Links. Fronted by Ron Dante, the lead singer of the fictional band The Archies. This sheet music is from 1969. 8.5" x 11", $10-15.

"98.6" – Keith. Keith's real name is James Barry Keefer. The sheet music for this number seven song was printed in January of 1967. 8.5" x 11", $10-20.

"Out in the Streets" – The Shangri-Las. Popular girl group better known for their single "Leader of the Pack." This song is a later release from 1965. 8.5" x 11", $20-40.

"Johnny Angel" – Shelley Fabares. This 1962 number one single was recorded by Fabares while she still held the role of Mary Stone in *The Donna Reed Show*. 9" x 12", $35-50.

"Ode to Billy Joe" – Bobbie Gentry. This 1967 country song is more about the apathetic way the family discusses the death of Billy Joe McAllister than why he jumped off the Tallahatchee Bridge in the first place. The back cover has a bio of Bobbie Gentry and mentions that the song was recorded in less than an hour. 9" x 12", $7-12.

"Yummy, Yummy, Yummy" – The Ohio Express. Unusual cover layout with the title printed twice and the band photo facing sideways. Printed in June of 1968. 8.5" x 11", $10-20.

"Beg, Borrow & Steal" – The Ohio Express. First release for this group; it charted as high as number twenty-nine in 1967. 8.5" x 11", $7-12.

"Chewy, Chewy" – The Ohio Express. In keeping with their bubblegum image, the band released this cute song in 1968. 9" x 12", $10-15.

"Beyond the Sea" – Bobby Darin. The late Bobby Darin entered the charts with this song at the very beginning of the decade, January 1960. 9" x 12", $10-15.

"The Loco-Motion" – Little Eva. This 1962 chart topper was originally recorded as a demo song; music mogul Don Kirshner liked the song enough to release it without having it re-recorded. The word "loco" in the title has the letters jumbled up, adding to the lively feel of the song. 8.5" x 11", $30-50.

"It's a Happening World" – The Tokens. Late, low charting single for this band from New York. The sheet music was printed in August 1967. 8.5" x 11", $15-30.

"Rhythm Of the Rain" (U.K.) – The Cascades. The Cascades, a San Diego based group, did exceptionally well with this song, reaching the top five in both the U.S. and Britain in 1963. 8.5" x 11", $15-20.

"B'wa Nina" – The Tokens. This song was released as a follow up to "The Lion Sleeps Tonight." The sheet music is rare and shows an early picture of the group in their prime. The title translates to "Pretty Girl." 8.5" x 11", $20-35.

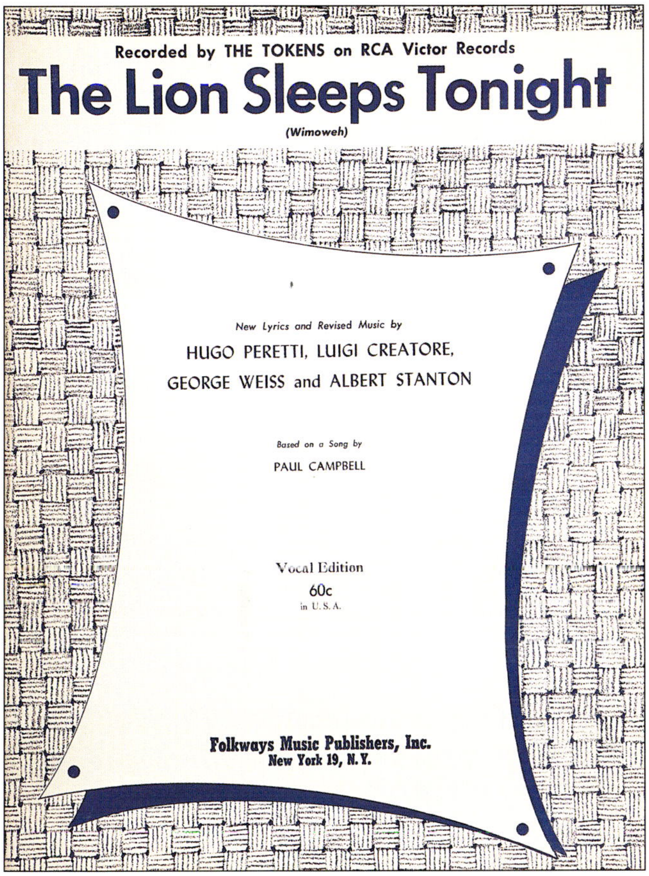


"The Lion Sleeps Tonight" – The Tokens. Huge hit for The Tokens in 1961. It was adapted from a South African folk song originally known as Wimoweh. Unfortunately, the sheet music for this classic early 1960s song was released without a photo of the band. 9" x 12", $15-30.

"Cherry, Cherry" – Neil Diamond. The cover of his first big hit shows a young Diamond in a brooding pose. Diamond also composed songs for The Monkees, including "I'm a Believer." 9" x 12", $15-25.

"You Got to Me" – Neil Diamond. Singer-songwriter Diamond got to number eighteen with "You Got To Me" in 1967. 9" x 12", $15-25.

"Smile a Little Smile For Me" – The Flying Machine. Appropriately themed cover for a band called The Flying Machine. This sheet is from late 1969 and had an original selling price of 95¢. 9" x 12", $15-20.

"This Guy's In Love With You" (U.K.) – Herb Alpert. A rare vocal performance by Alpert, who was known for instrumentals. The song was written by the duo of Burt Bacharach and Hal David and went all the way to number one in 1968. 8.5" x 11", $10-15.

"A Boy Named Sue" – Johnny Cash. Johnny Cash reached number two on the pop charts with this 1969 song written by famed author Shel Silverstein. 8.5" x 11", $10-15.

"Spanish Flea" – Herb Alpert. Alpert, one of the founders of A&M records, had a minor instrumental hit with this song in 1966. It went on to become the theme song for *The Dating Game*. 8.5" x 11", $10-15.

The 1910 Fruitgum Company was not actually a real band, rather a studio creation designed to record and release songs by producers Jeff Katz and Jerry Kasenetz. However, musicians were eventually assembled to play the music live in support of the albums. Sheet music from the 1910 Fruitgum Company represents some of the most colorful and dynamic pieces to come out of the 1960s. Since there was no "official" band, no group photo appears on them—which in this case, adds to the appeal. The photos shown here represent a complete collection of all the United States sheet music printed for The 1910 Fruitgum Company.

"May I Take a Giant Step (Into Your Heart?)" – 1910 Fruitgum Company. Bright and colorful cover drawing disguises the poor performance of this 1968 tune. 9" x 12", $10-15.

"1, 2, 3, Red Light" – 1910 Fruitgum Company. This 1968 song title was taken from the children's game of the same name. 9" x 12", $10-15.

"Goody Goody Gumdrops" – 1910 Fruitgum Company. Sugary-sweet bubblegum tune with an apple green and cotton candy pink cover. 9" x 12", $10-15.

"Special Delivery" – 1910 Fruitgum Company. This single only reached number thirty-eight on the pop charts in 1968. 9" x 12", $10-15.

"Simon Says" – 1910 Fruitgum Company. This song charted in both the U.S. (number four) and Britain (number two) and was the only song by this group to do so. Sheet music from the United Kingdom exists for "May I Take a Giant Step" in addition to this song. 9" x 12", $10-15.

"The Train" – 1910 Fruitgum Company. Only piece of sheet music for this group with a unique cover. Released in mid 1969, this was their last single. 9" x 12", $10-15.

"Indian Giver" – 1910 Fruitgum Company. You can hear the beat of Indian drums on this early 1969 song. 9" x 12", $10-15.

"Tie Me Kangaroo Down, Sport" – Rolf Harris. 1963 novelty song by Australian performer Rolf Harris. It mentions many animals native to his homeland such as koalas, cockatoos, and of course, kangaroos. 8.5" x 11", $10-20.

"Baby, I Love You" – Andy Kim. While Kim is best known for his number one song "Rock Me Gently," this song also did well by reaching the top ten in 1969. The cover makes interesting use of black and white imagery. 8.5" x 11", $10-20.

"Everybody's Talkin'" – Harry Nilsson. From the 1969 film *Midnight Cowboy*. The sheet music cover mentions recordings by five different artists, the most famous of which is that of Harry Nilsson. 9" x 12", $10-15.

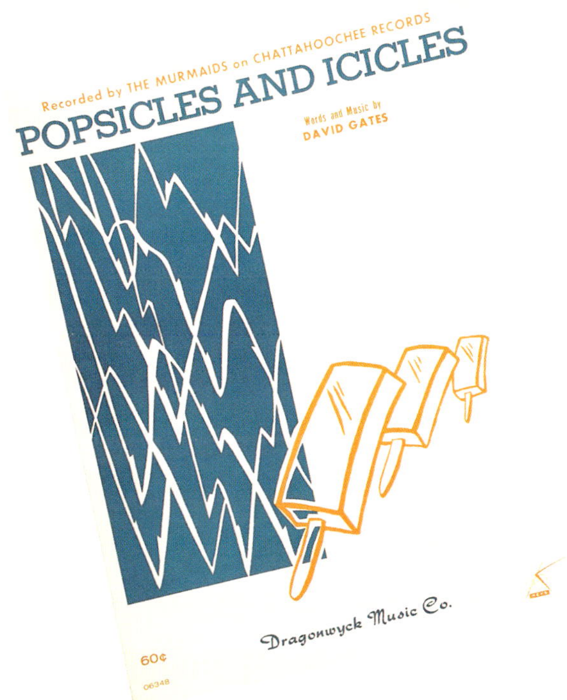


"Popsicles and Icicles" – The Murmaids. The group may have been only one-hit wonders, but the song still has the ability to evoke fond memories of a simpler time. Note that the cover uses specific popsicle and icicle images. 8.5" x 11", $20-30.

"Navy Blue" – Diane Renay. Appropriately blue cover includes a title with wavy lines mimicking seawater and a wistful photo of Renay as she dreams of her sailor. 9" x 12", $25-40.

"Wiwwian Wevy" – The Pastrami Malted. The 1968 novelty song "Wiwwian Wevy" was actually recorded by studio musicians and an already existing band was hired to portray the fictional Pastrami Malted. The band was expected to learn the song note for note so it could be performed live. It was one of the first (and possibly THE first) 45rpm records on the Metromedia label. 8.5" x 11", $10-20.

"Baby You Come Rollin' Across My Mind" – The Peppermint Trolley Company. This group, photographed here in peppermint striped pants, is the same group that recorded the original theme song to *The Brady Bunch*. This sheet is from June 1968. 8.5" x 11", $10-20.

"The Ballad of the Green Berets" – Sgt. Barry Sadler. Not just a number one song in 1966, but *the* number one song of 1966. Co-written by Sadler, it was a patriotic tribute to his fellow Green Berets. 9" x 12", very common, $7-12.

"Lil' Red Riding Hood" – Sam the Sham & The Pharaohs. While both songs rose to number two on the pop charts, the group is much more well known for "Wooly Bully" than for this 1966 song. 9" x 12", $15-30.

"Don't Wake Me Up in the Morning, Michael" – The Peppermint Rainbow. Follow up single to "Will You Be Staying After Sunday." Printed in July of 1969. 8.5" x 11", $10-20.

"Venus" – The Shocking Blue. This Dutch group just made it into the 1960s history books with this number one song that entered the Billboard® charts on December 13, 1969. 9" x 12", $15-25.

"Will You Be Staying After Sunday" – The Peppermint Rainbow. This sheet music was printed at two different times with the same cover. The original one shown here (from December 1968), has a glossy finish on a lightweight paper; the second, from April 1969, is printed on matte finish card stock. 8.5" x 11", $10-20.

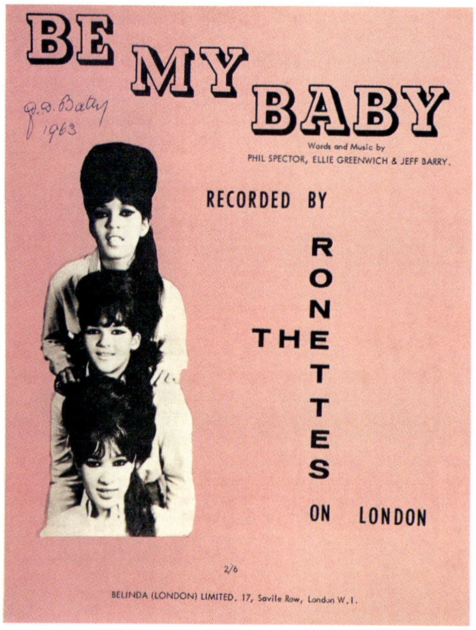


"Be My Baby" (U.K.) – The Ronettes. Using Phil Spector's "Wall of Sound" production, this 1963 song was the biggest of The Ronettes' career. 8.5" x 11", $15-20.

"Airplane Song (My Airplane)" – The Royal Guardsmen. In an attempt to depart from their novelty image, the band was dressed in suits for the cover of this 1967 sheet. 9" x 12", $10-15.

"Dizzy" – Tommy Roe. A number one song co-written by Tommy Roe, "Dizzy" was a bubblegum sounding composition and a complete departure from his earlier number one "Sheila," a rocker in the Buddy Holly tradition that was also written by Roe. This sheet was printed in February of 1969. 8.5" x 11", $10-15.

"Snoopy Versus the Red Baron" – The Royal Guardsmen. The Royal Guardsmen released no less than four Snoopy® themed songs, with this 1966 number two tune faring the best. 8.5" x 11", $15-20.

"Snoopy's Christmas" – The Royal Guardsmen. This holiday song managed to chart each December for three consecutive years beginning in 1967. 9" x 12", $10-15.

"Travelin' Man" – Ricky Nelson. Number one hit for the son of Ozzie and Harriet. 9" x 12", $20-30.

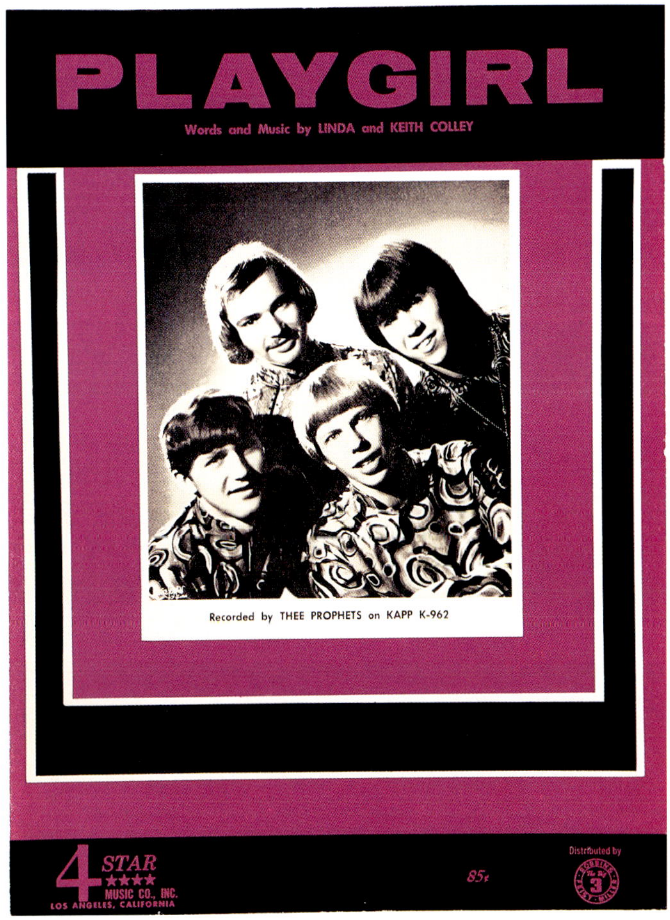


"Playgirl" – Thee Prophets. 1969 song from the band's only album, *Playgirl*. The extra 'e' in Thee is not an error—the group's name is spelled that way. 9" x 12", $10-15.

"Sam, You Made the Pants Too Long" – Barbara Streisand. Fun photo of Ms. Streisand dancing her way through this parody. The song did not do well at all, reaching only number ninety-eight in 1966. 9" x 12", $10-15.

"Sukiyaki" – Kyu Sakamoto. This Japanese song was originally titled "Ue O Muite Aruko," which translates to "I Look Up When I Walk." It was also released in an English version with the title "My First Lonely Night." The lyrics inside are written in both languages. The title of the song printed on this 1963 sheet music is misspelled. 8.5" x 11", $15-25.

"Thank U Very Much" (U.K.) – The Scaffold. Silly song that fared much better on the British charts than it did in America. The writer of this song, and one of the members of the group, is Michael McGear—also known as Michael McCartney, the brother of Beatle Paul. 8.5" x 11", $10-20.

"Harper Valley P.T.A." – Jeannie C. Riley. An accomplished country music artist, Ms. Riley managed to top the pop charts with this 1968 song. 8.5" x 11", $10-15.

"Roses Are Red" – Bobby Vinton. First and biggest hit for Vinton from 1962. The U.K. version of this sheet music uses an almost identical cover, but the photo is in black and white. 8.5" x 11", $7-12.

"Laurie (Strange Things Happen)" – Dickey Lee. Innocent picture of Lee on the cover veils a song that is really a ghost story. It tells the tale of a girl who comes back from the grave on her birthday a year after she passed away. This sheet was printed in June of 1965. 8.5" x 11", $10-20

"Na Na Hey Hey Kiss Him Goodbye" – Steam. Great cover drawing accompanies this 1969 song. No picture of the band was used since at the time of its release, no actual band called Steam existed. Once the song hit number one, a group of musicians were assembled to portray the band. 8.5" x 11", $7-12.

# Bibliography

*The Billboard Illustrated Encyclopedia of Rock*. New York, NY: Billboard Books, 2003.

Bronson, Fred. *The Billboard Book of Number One Hits*. New York, NY: Billboard Books, 1985.

Brown, Tony, Kutner, Jon & Warwick, Neil. *The Complete Book of the British Charts*. Great Britain: Omnibus Press, 2000.

Croft, Andrew. *Collecting Beatles Sheet Music & Songbooks*. Canada: Beatlology Magazine, 2003.

Dalley, Robert J. *Surfin' Guitars*. Ann Arbor, MI: Popular Culture, Ink., 1988, 1996.

Feldman, Christopher G. *The Billboard Book of No. 2 Singles*. New York, NY: Billboard Books, 2000.

Larkin, Colin. *The Virgin Encyclopedia of Sixties Music*. Great Britain: Virgin Books, 1997.

Mann, Brent. *99 Red Balloons and 100 Other All-Time Great One-Hit Wonders*. New York, NY: Kensington Publishing Corp. 2003.

Rees, Dafydd & Crampton, Luke. *Encyclopedia of Rock Stars*. New York, NY: DK Publishing, 1996.

Ritchie, John & Teel, John. *Rock 'N Roll Sheet Music*. Independent publisher, 2000.

Unterberger, Ritchie. *Turn! Turn! Turn! The 60's Folk-Rock Revolution*. San Francisco, CA: Backbeat Books, 2002.

Whitburn, Joel. *Billboard Top Pop Singles 1955-1999*. Menomonee Falls, WI: Record Research Inc., 2000.

Whitburn, Joel. *Top Pop Albums 1955-1992*. Menomonee Falls, WI: Record Research Inc., 1993.

http://www.allmusic.com

# Endnotes

[1]*http://wordnet.princeton.edu, ® 2.0, © 2003 Princeton University, "Sheet Music"*

[2]http://www.wikipedia.com, © 2000, 2001, 2002 Free Software Foundation, Inc., "Soul Music"

[3]http://www.allmusic.com, © 2005 All Media Guide, LLC., "Motown"

[4]http://www.allmusic.com, © 2005 All Media Guide, LLC., "British Invasion"

# Index

This index is divided into two parts, one listing all the song titles in the book and the other listing all the artists.

**By Song Title**

**By Artist**